SLICING, HOOKING and COOKING

SLICING, HOOKING
and
COOKING

GOURMET RECIPES
FOR
GOLFERS
and other good sports

Jackie Eddy

**RAINCOAST BOOK
DISTRIBUTION LTD.**

Jackie Eddy
12 Wellington Cres.
Edmonton, Alberta T5N 3V2

Editor: Mark Eric Miller
Design: Mario Carvajal/Grafika Art Studios
Cartoon Illustrator: Derek Carter
Photographer: Meg Best

Raincoast Book Distribution Ltd.,
15 West 6th Avenue
Vancouver, B.C.
V5Y 1K2

Canadian Cataloguing in Publication Data

Eddy, Jackie, 1931-
   Slicing, hooking and cooking

Includes index.
ISBN 0-920417-00-0

1. Cookery.   I. Title.   II. Title: Gourmet recipes
for golfers and other good sports.

TX652.E44   641.5   C80-094096-2

Printed and bound in Canada by T H Best Printing Co. Ltd.

Dedication

To my four children who are neglected not only while I am out golfing, but also while I am busy writing this book. They come home for lunch and want canned chicken noodle soup and peanut butter and banana sandwiches, but they have to have things like shrimp bisque and crab soufflé—not only once, but until I am satisfied with the results.

Acknowledgements

I would like to thank all the friends who have shared their recipes with me, and a particular thanks to George, Gracie, Marion, Mike, and Carolyn, who were all very supportive and helpful.

Table of Contents

Introduction

This book was written by an enthusiastic golfer who plans her meals around her golf games. But I think all who like to entertain will enjoy this book regardless of whether they play golf, entertain people who play golf, or entertain people who have never set foot on a golf course.

If you don't know anything about cooking, this book is not for you. Go out and get a copy of *Joy of Cooking*, which to me is the best basic cookbook on the market. If you know the basics and are looking for some new ideas, particularly in appetizers, soups, salads, and vegetable dishes, then you will enjoy this book.

Cooking has never been drudgery for me, it has always been fun. I was fortunate to grow up in a home where cooking was done with a great deal of love and affection and every meal was a happy occasion. Consequently, I have a great appreciation of good food which I hope to pass along to my daughters.

This book was conceived because I wanted to leave my girls an orderly collection of recipes that work and taste great. And when I took up golf at age forty, I was amazed at friends who got into an absolute tizzy when faced with having a dinner party on a golfing day. They could not believe that I would be on the golf course the same day I was expecting twenty people for dinner.

My idea grew, and while leaving my favorite tried and true recipes to my daughters, this book also offers some terrific 'make ahead' recipes and suggested menus for all people who like to entertain.

Cooking is definitely an art; it is a creative expression of yourself. Be imaginative, but only after you know the basics. It has taken many years of experimentation with recipes to arrive at the ones you will find on these pages.

Appetizers

Bacon and Cheese Appetizer

This is a good thing to have on hand during the golfing season. You can make tasty little snacks in less time than it takes to add up your golf score!

½ pound sharp Cheddar cheese, cut into chunks
10 slices raw bacon
1 medium onion, quartered
½ teaspoon dry mustard

Put all the ingredients through a grinder using a fine blade, or into a blender. Spread on bread rounds (Triscuits if time is short). Place under the broiler until they are golden brown. Serve hot. This mixture will keep for almost a week in the refrigerator but any leftover portion can be frozen.

Camembert and Butter Ball

Nobody ever knows what this is but they all want the recipe!

1 whole Camembert (including the skin)
equal amount of butter—maybe a wee bit more cheese than butter
1½ teaspoons finely chopped onion
paprika

In a food processor or blender, purée the Camembert and butter. Stir in the onion. Line a small bowl with plastic wrap and fill with the cheese mixture. Put into the fridge and let it sit all day or overnight. Unmold, remove the plastic wrap, and sprinkle with the paprika. Serve with squares of rye bread or water biscuits.

Caviar Pie

This recipe comes from a friend in California. I knew she wouldn't send me something that wasn't special and I was right. It is quite expensive to make but it is worth every penny. I serve a very small piece either with drinks before dinner or as a first course. This dish is really the most elegant, delicious, fantastic, exciting—I am running out of words to describe how good it is so I had better get on with the recipe.

Base:

6 hard-boiled eggs, finely chopped
½ medium onion, finely chopped
6 tablespoons melted butter
½ cup mayonnaise
½ teaspoon salt
dash white pepper
pinch of cayenne (red) pepper

Mix together the above base ingredients and place into a 6 inch pie plate. (Don't use a larger sized pie plate.) Cover with plastic wrap and chill overnight.

Topping:

½ cup sour cream (more to taste)
3½ ounce jar black lumpfish caviar, drained overnight (this is very important)
2 ounce jar red caviar
2 green onion tops, sliced
3 pimento-stuffed olives, sliced

Transfer the base egg mixture to a serving plate, invert and carefully remove the plastic wrap. Frost the top with the sour cream. Arrange a circle of sliced olives around the outside edge of the pie. Inside the olive ring, make a ring of lumpfish caviar. Inside the caviar ring, place a ring of green onion tops. Complete the pie by spreading the red caviar evenly over the remaining center space. Cut into wedges. Serves 12 to 14.

Liz's Cheese Ball

This is perfect for a large crowd.

6 ounces blue cheese
16 ounces cream cheese
10 ounces processed Cheddar cheese spread (comes in a jar)
2 tablespoons grated onion
1 teaspoon Worcestershire sauce
1 cup ground pecans
½ cup finely chopped parsley

Mix the cheeses which have been allowed to warm to room temperature. Add the onion, Worcestershire sauce, pecans, and parsley, and blend thoroughly. Shape into a ball and place into a bowl lined with plastic wrap. Chill overnight. Unmold and serve with crisp crackers.

Sue's Cheese and Chutney Ball

If you have homemade chutney on hand, use it, otherwise use H.P. Pickle Relish. This recipe can also be used as a hot hors d'oeuvre: spread some of the cheese ball on a Triscuit, put a very small dab of chutney in the center and place under the broiler until bubbly.

1 cup grated sharp Cheddar cheese
2 tablespoons sherry
¾ teaspoon curry powder
¼ teaspoon salt
8 ounces cream cheese
1 small jar of chutney (or H.P. Pickle Relish)

Mix all the ingredients together except the chutney, and place into a small bowl which has been lined with plastic wrap. Put into the refrigerator to chill. Unmold, remove the plastic wrap, and frost with the chutney. Serve with assorted crackers—Triscuits are best.

Tangy Cheese Balls

¼ cup butter
¼ cup Cheddar cheese
½ cup flour
¼ cup chopped ripe olives
paprika

Combine the butter and cheese. Blend in the flour and chopped ripe olives. Form into little balls. Sprinkle with paprika. Bake in a 400° oven for about 10 to 15 minutes, depending on the size of the balls. These may be prepared in advance and frozen before they are baked.

Cheese Squares

These are very popular, so make sure you have enough to go around.

1 small package cream cheese
5 ounces sharp Cheddar
½ cup butter
2 eggs
1 loaf unsliced bread, cut into 1-inch cubes (discard crusts)

Melt the cheeses and butter. Add the 2 egg yolks. Beat the 2 egg whites before folding into the mixture. Spread the mixture on all sides of the bread cubes (except the bottom). Put on a cookie sheet and freeze. When ready to serve, bake in a 350° oven until golden.

Cheese Wafers

There were one or two grandmothers (mothers of friends of mine) to whom I wanted to give a little something last year at Christmas. So I made little boxes of these cheese wafers and gave them along with a typewritten copy of the recipe. One of the grandmothers (who is one of my very favorite people in the whole world) said, "They were so good I kept them in my room and didn't even share them."

1 tub Imperial Cheddar cheese (comes in a flat round red container)
½ cup margarine
1 cup flour
1½ cups Rice Krispies
⅛ to ¼ teaspoon cayenne (red) pepper

Mix together the cheese, margarine, flour, and cayenne. Fold in the Rice Krispies. Roll into small balls and press with a fork—dip the fork into cold water first. Bake in a 350° oven for 12 to 15 minutes.

Crocked Cheese

2 cups finely grated old Cheddar cheese
½ cup Cheez Whiz
½ cup crumbled blue cheese
3 tablespoons port or good red wine

Combine the ingredients in a mixer and beat until smooth. Put into a crock and store in the fridge. Serve with crackers.

Clam Savories

These make a nice first course but I have also served them with drinks before dinner. Have an adequate napkin as the shells are hot.

4 tablespoons flour
4 tablespoons butter
1 cup milk
1 cup bread crumbs
¾ cup grated Cheddar cheese

¼ teaspoon dry mustard
1 tin baby clams or 2 tins minced
   (7 ounces), drained
salt and pepper to taste

Make a thick white sauce with the flour, butter, and milk. Add the bread crumbs, cheese, mustard, clams, salt, and pepper. Put this mixture into individual shells and leave in the refrigerator overnight. The next day, bake in a 300° oven for ¾ hour. Serves 4.

Curried Chicken Balls

2 chicken breasts
1 bay leaf
1 large onion
2 stalks celery
2 whole cloves

5 or 6 sprigs parsley
pinch rosemary, marjoram, and thyme
3 teaspoons curry powder, or to taste
1 teaspoon salt
mayonnaise (just to bind)
chopped buttered almonds

Simmer the chicken breasts with the bay leaf, onion, celery, cloves, parsley, rosemary, marjoram, and thyme. When tender, let cool in their own broth. Remove the chicken and grind through the finest blade of a food chopper. Bind the ground chicken with the mayonnaise and add the curry powder and salt to taste. Form into little balls and roll in chopped buttered almonds.

Curried Shrimp Puffs

¾ cup chopped cooked shrimp
½ cup mayonnaise
¼ teaspoon curry powder
1 egg white, beaten until stiff
toast squares or soda biscuits

A little salt may be required—some shrimp seem more salty than others, so taste them first. Beat the egg white until it is stiff, then fold in the rest of the ingredients. Pile on toast squares and put under the broiler until puffy and brown. When in a hurry, just use soda biscuits, they seem just as popular. Everything except the egg white can be assembled ahead of time.

Delicious Cocktail Wieners

Perfect for a large cocktail party. Have these weiners at one end of your table, and some sweet and sour meatballs—which you have made ahead and frozen—at the other end. Display a lot of flowers and nuts in between. (You may want to add some cheese and crackers.)

1 pound small cocktail wieners (or sausages)
1 small jar prepared mustard (6 ounces)
1 jar red currant jelly (9 ounces)

Boil the wieners. Combine the jelly and mustard in a saucepan. Stir and cook slowly until well blended, and bring to a boil. Boil 1 minute. Combine the sauce with the boiled wieners in a chafing dish. The sauce may be made ahead and reheated with the wieners.

Escargots

This garlic butter is sufficient for 24 escargots.

1 cup white wine
½ cup butter
4 green onions, finely chopped
½ teaspoon dry mustard

6 cloves garlic, minced
2 teaspoons Worcestershire sauce
4 tablespoons chopped parsley
½ cup bread crumbs

Soak the snails all day in white wine. Mix together the butter, green onions, mustard, garlic, Worcestershire sauce, and chopped parsley. Put a bit of this garlic butter into each escargot shell, then a snail, then more garlic butter. Sprinkle the bread crumbs on top of the butter. Bake in a 350° oven for 15 minutes.

Joyce's Golden Olive Nuggets

1 cup grated sharp Cheddar cheese
¼ cup butter
1 teaspoon celery seed
¾ cup flour
8 ounces large stuffed green olives

Blend the cheese, butter, and celery seed. Stir in the flour and knead well to form dough. Drain the olives well on paper towels. Mold the cheese dough around the olives, about 1 teaspoon per olive. Bake at 400° for about 15 minutes.

Marinated Shrimp

2 pounds shrimp, cooked
1 lemon, thinly sliced
1 small white Spanish onion,
  thinly sliced
½ cup pitted black olives, well drained
2 tablespoons chopped pimento
½ cup fresh lemon juice
¼ cup oil

1 tablespoon wine vinegar
1 clove garlic, minced
½ bay leaf, crumbled
1 tablespoon dry mustard
¼ teaspoon cayenne pepper
1 teaspoon salt
freshly ground black pepper to taste

Put the shrimp into a serving dish. Add the sliced lemon, onion, olives, and pimento. Toss them together. In a jar, combine the lemon juice, wine vinegar, oil, garlic, bay leaf, mustard, cayenne pepper, salt, and pepper. Shake well and stir into the shrimp. Cover and refrigerate overnight—or make it in the morning. Stir occasionally while it is marinating in the refrigerator. The shrimp can be served on individual small plates or shells.

Meat Empanadas

Both this recipe and the following one for Meat Samosa are a little time consuming but they can be made ahead and frozen.

Make the pastry for Meat Samosa (see following recipe) or use your own favorite pastry recipe.

Filling:

2 cloves garlic, minced
1 green pepper, finely chopped
1 pound ground round steak
½ cup tomato purée or paste
1 teaspoon salt

3 tablespoons dry red wine
2 tablespoons capers
2 tablespoons diced olives
3 teaspoons chili powder
¼ teaspoon Tabasco sauce

Sauté the garlic, pepper, and beef until tender. Add the tomato paste, salt, and wine, and let cook until the liquid evaporates. Add the capers, olives, chili powder, and Tabasco. Let cool. Cut the dough into circles 2 inches in diameter. Place a spoonful of filling into the center of each circle and fold over. Press the edges together with a fork to seal. Place on a cookie sheet and bake in a 425° oven for 20 minutes.

Meat Samosa

Filling:

6 tablespoons margarine
1 large onion, finely chopped
2 cloves garlic, minced
1 pound lean ground beef
1 teaspoon coriander
½ teaspoon salt

¼ teaspoon pepper
1 teaspoon curry powder
½ teaspoon cumin
2 teaspoons dried red pepper
½ cup water
½ cup sour cream

Heat the margarine in a skillet. Add the onion and garlic and cook for 3 minutes. Add the meat and cook until it shows no more sign of pink. Add all the other ingredients and cook until the moisture is absorbed. Cool.

Pastry:

2 cups flour
¼ teaspoon salt
2 tablespoons sour cream
1 tablespoon margarine
½ cup cold water

Combine the flour, salt, margarine, sour cream, and about ½ cup of cold water. The dough should be slightly softer than a pie crust dough. Knead well. Break off dough the size of a walnut and roll into a thin circle about 3½ inches in diameter. Cut each circle in half. Top each half with a tablespoon of filling and fold each side in to form a triangle. Moisten the edges with cold water and seal. Fry in deep fat at 375° until golden brown. Serve hot.

Oat Biscuits

This recipe comes from the 1977 Edmonton Ladies' Golf Champion, Lise Vautour, who likes to serve these instead of crackers with cheese. She insists they are more healthy. They are also very tasty and an attractive addition to any cheese tray.

3 cups instant oats
1 teaspoon salt
1 teaspoon baking powder
½ cup oil
½ cup hot water
¼ cup whole wheat flour

Mix the ingredients and roll out thinly on a floured board. Cut into tiny rounds—use a liqueur glass. Bake in a 350° oven for about 10 minutes.

Onion Squares

This recipe is great because you always have the ingredients on hand. If friends drop in unexpectedly and can be 'persuaded' to stay for a drink, you can always whip up this tasty hors d'oeuvre in a hurry.

bread slices
onion slices
mayonnaise
Parmesan cheese

Cut (day old) bread into bite-sized squares. Place a thin slice of the onion on the bread squares. Top with a dab of mayonnaise. Sprinkle with the cheese. Place under the broiler until brown. Serve at once.

Oysters Rockefeller

A beautiful first course.

1½ pounds spinach
2 teaspoons grated onion
4 tablespoons butter
4 tablespoons flour
2 cups light cream
1 tablespoon lemon juice

pinch of nutmeg
garlic salt and white pepper to taste
1 pint oysters
½ cup buttered bread crumbs
2 tablespoons Parmesan cheese

Wash the spinach and cook in a little salted boiling water until just tender. Drain well and chop finely. Sauté the onion in 4 tablespoons of melted butter. Add the flour. Gradually stir in the cream. Cook until the mixture thickens then add the lemon juice, nutmeg, garlic, salt, and pepper. Reserve ½ cup of this cream sauce. To the remaining 1½ cups of sauce, add the chopped spinach. Divide this spinach mixture equally among 8 individual shells. Place the oysters on top. Place a spoonful of the remaining ½ cup of cream sauce on top of the oysters. Mix the bread crumbs and Parmesan cheese and sprinkle on top of the shells. Bake in a 350° oven for about 20 to 25 minutes.

Country Pâté

We were entertaining a group of doctors from across the country one time and I served this pâté. One doctor from Montreal told me it was the best he had ever tasted. Enough said.

bacon to line a baking dish
1 pound chicken livers
4 tablespoons butter
4 eggs, hard-boiled
1 onion
2 cloves garlic
1 pound mildly seasoned sausage meat

2 tablespoons brandy
½ teaspoon allspice
1 teaspoon salt
½ teaspoon rosemary
½ teaspoon freshly ground black pepper
2 tablespoons flour

Line a glass loaf dish with strips of bacon. Gently sauté the chicken livers in the butter. Put them through the fine blade of a meat grinder with the eggs, onion, garlic, and sausage meat. (A blender will not do, as it alters the texture.) Combine the mixture with the brandy, allspice, salt, rosemary, pepper, and flour. Pour this mixture into the glass loaf dish and cover with aluminum foil. Sit the dish in hot water and bake in a 350° oven for 1½ to 2 hours or until the liquid in the pan is clear. Cool for 15 minutes. Pour off any fat. Weight the pâté with a brick or any other heavy object and cool completely in the refrigerator. To serve, unmold and remove excess fat. Pass with thin, hot toast. For a first course, serve the pâté sliced on leaves of baby lettuce and pass a sauceboat of Cumberland sauce (see index). This keeps very well—it can be made several days before serving and still be delicious when served.

Pâté à la Maison

For those of you who prefer a smooth pâté, this is it. Perfect for the golfing season because you use a blender and it takes very little time, providing it is the type of blender with the wide bottom.

½ pound chicken livers
2 tablespoons butter
2 hard-boiled eggs
6 ounces cream cheese
2 tablespoons brandy
salt and freshly ground pepper to taste

In a saucepan cook the ½ pound of chicken livers in the 2 tablespoons of melted butter, stirring for about 10 minutes or until they are tender. Blend the livers and the eggs a little at a time in the container of the blender. Beat the 6 ounces of cream cheese until soft and combine with the liver mixture in the blender. Blend the mixture until smooth. Add the brandy and salt and pepper to taste. Pack in a crock and chill thoroughly. Serve with unsalted crackers or thin squares of rye bread.

Pâté for Those Who Hate Liver

I am sure you have friends who ask when you serve pâté, "Does this have liver in it?" If the answer is yes, they will pass. This recipe is for those friends, and it is delicious.

1½ pounds ground pork
1½ cups bread crumbs
1½ cups milk
3 cloves garlic, minced finely
½ teaspoon ground cloves
salt and pepper to taste

Mix together well all the ingredients and simmer very slowly for two hours. Put into a blender or through a meat grinder if no blender is available. Put into crocks and cool. Serve with toast rounds or small pieces of fresh French bread.

Pickled Mushrooms

These disappear very quickly, often before the party for which they were intended—that is, if your family likes to snack!

⅔ cup tarragon vinegar, or wine vinegar with pinch dried tarragon
1 medium clove garlic, crushed
1 tablespoon sugar
½ cup salad oil
2 tablespoons water
1½ teaspoons salt
freshly ground pepper to taste
dash Tabasco sauce
1 medium onion, thinly sliced and separated into rings
2 pints fresh mushrooms—leave small ones whole, cut large ones into halves or quarters

Combine the first 8 ingredients to make a marinade. Put into a plastic bag with the mushrooms and sliced onion. The plastic bag makes it easier to mix—just shake the bag gently several times. Seal the bag with a twist-tie and chill overnight. Before serving, shake the bag several times to distribute the marinade. Drain and serve as appetizers (with toothpicks).

Pickled Mushrooms with Cherry Tomatoes

The preceding recipe can be used without the sliced onion by substituting ½ to 1 pound of cherry tomatoes. Don't add the cherry tomatoes until about 4 hours before serving them. Slip the cherry tomatoes into boiling water for 5 seconds then plunge them into cold water. The skins will slip off easily. Add them to the bag containing the mushrooms and marinade. When ready to serve, drain and sprinkle with chopped green onions. Serve with toothpicks.

Smoked Salmon Rolls

A very elegant way to start a meal—can also be served as a first course.

2 cups cooked shrimp, coarsely chopped
½ cup cream, whipped
1 tablespoon horseradish
salt and white pepper to taste
12 slices smoked salmon

Gently mix together the shrimp, whipped cream, horseradish, salt, and pepper. Divide this mixture among the 12 slices of smoked salmon. Roll the smoked salmon into cornets and arrange them on a bed of shredded soft lettuce, such as Boston or leaf lettuce. Serve 2 per person and garnish with slices of lemon. Serves 6.

Spinach Dip for Raw Vegetables

This is a great dip for the raw vegetable enthusiasts—there are fresh vegetables even in the dip itself.

1 cup chopped spinach
½ cup chopped parsley
1 teaspoon salt
1 teaspoon freshly ground pepper
½ cup finely chopped chives or green onions
2 cups mayonnaise, thinned with a little cream

Blend all the ingredients in a blender or food processor. Serve this sauce well chilled. Serve as an appetizer with a cold fresh vegetable tray including carrot, celery, and zucchini sticks, pieces of raw cauliflower and raw broccoli, whole mushrooms, and cherry tomatoes.

Soups

Beef, Vegetable, and Barley Soup

This soup is made with beef shank rather than soup bones, and once it is trimmed and cubed there is no fat, so it is not necessary to let the soup sit overnight.

3 pounds beef shank
6 cups water
1 cup tomato juice
2 beef bouillon cubes
1 large onion, diced
½ cup diced celery

½ cup diced carrots
2 cups shredded cabbage
1 teaspoon salt
¼ teaspoon chili powder
1 teaspoon Worcestershire sauce
2 tablespoons pot barley

Remove the meat from the bone and cut into small cubes. Brown it well. Put the meat along with the bone and all other ingredients into a soup kettle. Cover and simmer for two hours. Remove the bone before serving. Serves 8.

Boola Boola Soup

I first tasted this soup at the Calgary Inn when it had just opened, and I thought it was excellent. The menu described the soup, I suppose because nobody would order a soup with that name without some idea of what was in it. The menu described the soup as green pea, turtle, and sherry. As soon as I got home, I rushed out to buy the pea soup and the turtle soup with the hope that I might be able to duplicate this recipe. It is difficult to carry an exact taste in one's mind just as it is difficult to carry a particular color, but to me it seemed almost identical in flavor and so simple to make, I couldn't believe it.

1 can turtle soup (10 ounces)
1 can green pea soup (10 ounces)
1 tablespoon sherry, or to taste
1 tablespoon whipped cream per serving

Mix the soups together. Add the sherry to taste. Heat, and just before serving, add the 1 tablespoon of whipped cream to each soup cup and place under the broiler until golden brown. Serves 4.

Brown Soup

The first time I served this soup, one of the dinner guests liked it so much she asked if she could come back in the morning and have the rest for breakfast.

4 tablespoons butter	1 cup red wine
4 onions, sliced thinly	2 eggs
3 tablespoons flour	3 tablespoons heavy cream
6 cups stock or 2 cans consommé	2 tablespoons chopped parsley
and 2½ cans water	1 teaspoon chopped chives

Melt the butter in a deep saucepan. Add the onions and sauté until very brown, about 15 minutes, stirring frequently. Sprinkle with the flour and stir well. Gradually add the stock, stirring constantly until the boiling point is reached. Add the wine and cook over low heat for 1 hour. Correct the seasoning. In a separate bowl, beat together the eggs, cream, parsley, and chives. To this mixture, gradually add 1 cup of the hot soup, stirring constantly to prevent curdling. Return the mixture to the saucepan, stirring well. Heat thoroughly but do not allow to boil. Serves 6.

Chicken Velvet Soup

Easy!

4 eggs
4 tablespoons sherry
2 tablespoons lemon juice
4 cups hot chicken broth (almost boiling)
salt and pepper to taste
chopped parsley

In a blender combine the eggs, sherry, and lemon juice. Blend for about 15 seconds. Remove the cover and with the motor still running, slowly pour in the hot chicken stock. Season with salt and pepper to taste. Garnish with chopped parsley. This soup can be made the day before and reheated, but do not let it boil. Serves 4.

Note: The chicken broth has to be hot enough to 'cook' the eggs.

Clam Chowder

6 tablespoons butter
1 large onion, chopped
1 large carrot, grated
1 large celery stalk, grated
2 tablespoons chopped parsley
8 to 10 tablespoons flour
4 cups milk
1 small can evaporated milk

1 large potato, diced
1 can large butter clams, including juice
2 cans baby clams, including juice
1 cup light cream
½ teaspoon salt
¼ teaspoon white pepper
¼ teaspoon paprika
1 teaspoon seafood seasoning

Melt the butter in a Dutch oven or other large pot. Sauté the onion, carrot, celery, and parsley until the onion is soft but not brown—about 5 to 10 minutes. Stir in the flour. Gradually add the milk and evaporated milk, stirring constantly. Cook until this mixture thickens. Peel and dice the potato and, in a separate small saucepan, cook it in the juice from the can of large clams. When the potato is soft add it to the above mixture, including the clam juice. Chop the large clams coarsely and add to the above along with the 2 cans of baby clams. Stir in the cream and correct the seasoning. Heat but do not boil or the cream will curdle. Sauté the paprika and seafood seasoning in a little bit of butter and add at the last minute. Do not stir—this will float on top and make an attractive garnish. Serves 10 to 12.

Cream of Fresh Pea Soup

You cannot substitute canned peas into this recipe. As far as I am concerned, there are very few times you CAN substitute canned peas for the fresh or freshly frozen. Frozen peas can be used in this recipe, but I prefer to wait until summer for the fresh ones. This was my dad's favorite cream soup. Years ago there was no such thing as frozen peas, so we were only treated to this soup in the summer.

3 cups fresh peas, shelled
1½ cups water
3 cups cream
3 egg yolks, beaten
2 tablespoons butter
salt and pepper to taste

Cook the peas in a double boiler in 1½ cups water. Put into a blender or force through a sieve. Put the cream into a pot and when heated, add the purée of peas, and salt and pepper to taste. Cook 5 minutes, stirring constantly. Add the egg yolks, making sure to add a little of the hot mixture to the yolks first, so they won't curdle. Whisk them into the pea/cream mixture. Add the butter, folding it in until it is melted. Serves 6.

Cream of Spinach and Oyster Soup

This recipe comes from a super golfer, and super is the best way to describe this soup!

9 fresh oysters (an 8 ounce container of frozen oysters is about the right size)
4 tablespoons cooked spinach
½ cup cream
2 tablespoons butter, melted
½ teaspoon Accent
dash of garlic salt
pinch of nutmeg
salt and white pepper to taste
¾ pint milk
1 tablespoon cornstarch
whipped cream for garnish (lightly salted)

Blend the drained oysters, spinach, cream, butter, and seasonings in a blender for about 15 seconds. Heat the milk. Add the spinach and oyster mixture and bring gently to the simmering point, being careful not to boil. Add the cornstarch which has been mixed to a smooth paste with some of the warm milk. Cook, stirring constantly until thickened. Put into individual heat proof soup dishes and top with lightly whipped cream—1 tablespoon per dish should be sufficient as it will spread when heated. Season the cream with a pinch of salt. Put under the broiler until glazed. Serves 4 to 6.

Crème Crécy: Cream of Carrot Soup

3 tablespoons butter
½ onion, chopped
1 pound finely chopped carrots
2 pints chicken stock
2 tablespoons uncooked rice
salt and pepper to taste
6 tablespoons heavy cream

Melt 2 tablespoons of the butter in a heavy saucepan. Add the onions. Cook, stirring occasionally, about 5 minutes or until the onions are soft but not brown. Add the carrots, chicken stock, and rice. Simmer gently, uncovered, for 30 minutes until the carrots are cooked. Put the soup through a sieve into a clean saucepan, or put into a blender for 20 to 30 seconds until smooth. Reheat and season with salt and pepper. Stir in the cream and the remaining 1 tablespoon of butter. Serves 6.

French Onion Soup

When my husband and I were first married, we were fortunate to live in Montreal for three years. At that time, twenty-three years ago, it had the best restaurants in Canada, of which we took full advantage. It was then that I was first introduced to French onion soup and it has been a favorite ever since.

5 cups thinly sliced onions
½ clove garlic, minced
3 tablespoons butter
1 tablespoon oil
2 quarts boiling brown stock (canned beef bouillon can be used, diluted according to directions on the can)
½ cup vermouth (optional)
½ teaspoon salt
freshly ground black pepper to taste
thin rounds hard-toasted French bread (if bread is thick it absorbs too much of the broth)
1 cup grated Mozzarella cheese
1 cup grated Swiss cheese
Parmesan cheese, for sprinkling on top

In a heavy, 4 quart, covered saucepan, slowly cook the onions and garlic in the butter and oil until they are a rich brown color—do not burn. This will take about 20 minutes. Stir occasionally at first but once the onions start to brown, watch them carefully. Add the stock and simmer for about 30 minutes. If vermouth is to be added, add it at this time. Correct the seasoning. Ladle into individual oven-proof soup dishes. Place a piece of the toasted French bread on top and cover generously with a mixture of Mozzarella and Swiss cheese. Sprinkle with the Parmesan cheese and place under the broiler until the cheese is brown and bubbly. Serves 8.

Onion Soufflé Soup

For a real gourmet touch serve the previous soup recipe, but instead of putting the grated cheese on top of the toasted French bread, try this soufflé topping.

¾ pint thick cream sauce
6 tablespoons freshly grated Swiss Gruyère cheese
2 egg whites, stiffly beaten

Stir the Swiss cheese into the cream sauce, and fold in the stiffly beaten egg whites. Spoon one or two tablespoons of this soufflé topping over the French toast and bake in a hot oven (450°) for 8 to 10 minutes or until the soufflé has risen and is golden.

Gazpacho

This soup is commonly referred to as the 'salad soup' and is perfect for hot summer weather.

4 cups chopped tomatoes
1½ cups chopped green pepper
¾ cup chopped onion
1 clove garlic, minced
2 cups consommé
1 tablespoon paprika
freshly ground black pepper to taste

½ cup lemon juice
¼ cup olive oil
1 teaspoon salt
½ teaspoon ground cumin
½ cup finely diced cucumber
½ cup finely diced green pepper
½ cup finely diced green onion

Put all the ingredients into a blender except the ½ cup green pepper, ½ cup diced cucumber, and ½ cup diced green onion. Blend for 2 to 3 minutes. Put into the fridge and chill well, for at least 4 hours. Serve the chopped cucumber, green pepper, and green onion in separate dishes. Serves 8.

Lynn's Pumpkin Soup

We first discovered this soup in Jamaica several years ago and wondered why it was not more popular here. It's delicious. We serve it as part of our Thanksgiving dinner and it is popular with adults and children alike.

2 tablespoons butter
½ cup minced onion
½ cup minced celery
1 cup pumpkin purée (may be canned)
1 cup mashed potatoes

3 tins chicken broth, or 3½ cups chicken stock or bouillon
½ teaspoon mace
½ cup heavy cream
salt and white pepper to taste

In the 2 tablespoons of butter, sauté the onion and celery for about 5 minutes. Add the pumpkin purée, the mashed potatoes, the chicken stock, and the mace. Use a whisk to make sure there are no lumps. Simmer for 15 minutes. Remove from the heat and add the heavy cream, salt, and pepper. Return to the heat but do not let the soup boil. Serve in heated bowls and garnish with chopped chives or parsley. Serves 6.

Navy Bean Soup

I don't serve soup too often during the golfing season, but then this cookbook was not intended to be used just during the golfing season!

1 pound dried white beans
1 ham bone
2 tablespoons butter, or ham fat
3 medium onions, chopped
2 cloves garlic, minced

6 stalks celery, chopped
1 cup cooked mashed potatoes
¼ cup chopped parsley
salt and pepper to taste
dash of Tabasco sauce

Soak the beans covered in cold water overnight. Drain the beans and put them into a soup kettle with 3 quarts of water, or enough to cover them. Add the ham bone with some meat on it. Sauté the onions, garlic, and celery in a bit of ham fat if you have it, if not use about 2 tablespoons of butter. Add the sautéed vegetables to the pot with the remaining ingredients. Simmer for 3 to 4 hours. Remove the ham bone, dice the meat, and return the meat to the soup before serving. Serves 8 to 10.

Shrimp Bisque with Shrimp Balls

*This is a marvelous 'make ahead' gourmet soup. I make the soup the day
before and reheat it just before serving time. The shrimp balls I also make
ahead and they freeze well. My son's favorite lunch is the Japanese instant
dried noodle soup with some green peas and shrimp balls thrown in. Don't add
the shrimp balls until just before serving.*

1 large potato
1 tin (10 ounces) cream of shrimp soup
1 cup light cream
1 cup milk
salt and pepper to taste
chopped parsley for garnish

Cook 1 large potato cut into cubes. When cooked, drain and add to the rest of
the ingredients. Put everything into a blender (except the parsley) and blend for
20 seconds. Heat and serve with the shrimp balls (recipe as follows). Add a few
to each soup plate just before serving along with a pinch of chopped parsley.
Serves 4. If doubling this recipe, double everything except the cream.

Shrimp Balls for Bisque:

1 tablespoon butter
½ onion, chopped
1 tablespoon minced green pepper
1½ teaspoons minced parsley
½ pound cooked shrimp, finely chopped
¼ cup bread crumbs
1 egg yolk
paprika

This shouldn't need salt as the shrimp are usually salty enough. Melt the butter
in a skillet. Add the onion, green pepper, and parsley. Sauté slowly until the
onion is cooked. Add the shrimp, bread crumbs, and egg yolk. Taste for salt and
add salt at this time if it is needed. Shape into balls the size of marbles. Sprinkle
with paprika and put into a moderate oven for about 10 minutes. Makes about
36 tiny balls.

Soupe au Pistou: Garlic Vegetable Soup

*This French soup, of which there are many regional varieties, is substantial
enough to serve as a meal in itself.*

½ cup navy beans (soaked overnight)
1 tablespoon olive oil
1 onion, chopped
5 cups chicken bouillon
½ pound green beans
2 zucchini, chopped
1 carrot, chopped
1 leek, sliced

2 potatoes, diced
1 teaspoon salt, or to taste
pepper to taste
3 cloves garlic
½ teaspoon basil
2 egg yolks
¼ cup olive oil
Parmesan cheese

Boil the navy beans until tender, then drain. Heat the oil in a large saucepan and
fry the onion until it turns golden. Add the chicken bouillon and bring to a boil.
Add the cooked and drained navy beans, green beans, zucchini, carrot, leek,
potatoes, salt, and pepper. Bring to a boil and cook until the vegetables are
tender, about 10 minutes. Put the garlic through a press and mix with the basil
and egg yolks. Very gradually add the ¼ cup of olive oil to the garlic, basil, and
egg yolk mixture, a few drops at a time as when making mayonnaise. Stir
carefully into the soup. Cook gently for 5 minutes, stirring occasionally. Serve at
once. Pass the Parmesan cheese separately. Serves 8.

Tomato Bouillon

*This is an ideal soup to serve before an otherwise rich meal. Start with a thin
soup such as this, end with a fruit dessert, and you can afford some of those
calories in the middle. (If you use Sugar Twin instead of the sugar called for in
the recipe, there are only 35 calories per cup.)*

40 ounces Clamato juice
2 tins consommé
1 cup water
sprinkle of white pepper to taste
4 teaspoons sugar
4 teaspoons cornstarch
¼ cup cold water

Simmer the first 5 ingredients together for 5 minutes. Mix the cornstarch and
water and stir into the heated mixture, boiling until clear (20 to 30 minutes).
Serves 6 to 8.

Wild Mushroom Soup

We are fortunate to live in an area where wild mushrooms grow. If you know anything about wild mushrooms, you know they are far superior to cultivated ones but quite unpredictable. They happen to grow in certain areas of our golf course—just a few of us know the edible ones and we are not telling! This year, to everyone's dismay, there were hardly any, but about 10 years ago there was a bumper crop. We picked POUNDS. I froze some—they don't freeze well unless you cook them first. I dried some—a tedious process. I pickled some, made soup, soufflés, mushroom pies, vegetable casseroles—you name it. We had so many just sautéed in butter (which is the very best way to prepare them), that I could afford to experiment. I came up with this Wild Mushroom Soup recipe which is absolutely delicious.

½ pound wild mushrooms
2 tablespoons butter
2 tablespoons flour
1½ quarts chicken broth
1 can cream of mushroom soup
½ cup heavy cream
chopped parsley

Wash the mushrooms and chop them finely. Sauté them in butter until fairly soft. Sprinkle with the flour, stirring constantly. Add the chicken broth gradually and simmer for ½ hour. Strain the mushroom soup and add it to the above mixture. Return to simmer for another 2 to 3 minutes. Add the cream. Heat thoroughly but do not boil. When ready to serve, pour into a hot soup tureen or individual soup plates or bouillon cups and sprinkle with chopped parsley. Serves 6 to 8.

Salads

Avocado Ring

1 envelope gelatin
¼ cup cold water
1 cup mashed avocado
½ cup mayonnaise
3 tablespoons lemon juice
2 tablespoons lime juice
1 teaspoon salt
½ cup whipping cream

Soften the gelatin in cold water, then dissolve over hot water. Combine with the other ingredients. Fold in the whipped cream. Pour this mixture into an oiled mold and chill until firm. The ring may be filled with seafood for a luncheon dish.

'Bean' Bean Salad

This salad is very colorful, with white beans, green pepper and red pimento. It is also a very good source of vegetable protein.

1 pound small navy beans
½ cup chopped green pepper
½ cup chopped onion
½ cup chopped celery
2 ounces pimentos, chopped
½ cup salad oil
¼ cup cider vinegar
2 tablespoons sugar
1 teaspoon salt
½ teaspoon freshly ground black pepper
½ teaspoon basil

Soak the beans overnight. Cover them with water and simmer until tender. Drain well and let them cool. Add the green pepper, onion, celery, and pimentos. Make a dressing with the remaining ingredients and pour it over the vegetables. Mix well. Chill several hours before serving. Serves 10 to 12.

Bean Sprout and Spinach Salad

Very healthy, very tasty, very different.

1 cup fresh bean sprouts (canned won't do)
½ pound spinach (or more)
½ cup thinly sliced water chestnuts

Wash the bean sprouts and drain thoroughly. Wash and dry the spinach leaves. Arrange the spinach leaves in a salad bowl. Top with the bean sprouts and water chestnuts. Toss with Sesame Seed Dressing (see page 53).

Caesar Salad

I must admit this is my favorite salad in the whole world. I never tire of it and never fail to order it when eating out. The best one I ever had was at a restaurant in San Francisco. The charge for the Caesar salad was $7.50, which automatically caught my attention! I decided to splurge and I was not disappointed. Watching very carefully I noticed everything was the same as the traditional recipe except for 2 teaspoons of the chef's ingredient X, the contents of which he was not about to divulge. However, I think the following recipe is ALMOST as good.

1 clove garlic
¼ teaspoon salt
6 anchovies
6 capers
2 egg yolks
dash of Worcestershire sauce
dash of Tabasco sauce
pinch of dry mustard

5 tablespoons olive oil
2½ tablespoons red wine vinegar
½ lemon
1 large head romaine lettuce
½ cup Parmesan cheese
croutons
freshly ground pepper

Crush a clove of garlic in a large salad bowl. Add ¼ teaspoon salt and rub the bowl with a piece of waxed paper. Crush 4 of the anchovies and all the capers with a fork to make a paste. Add the egg yolks, dash of Worcestershire sauce, dash of Tabasco sauce, and small pinch of mustard. Start adding the oil very slowly, stirring constantly with a fork. It should have a mayonnaise-like consistency. Now add the vinegar, again a little at a time stirring constantly. Add the lemon juice. Tear up the lettuce and place on top of this dressing. Toss lightly. Cut up the remaining two anchovies and add to the lettuce with the Parmesan cheese and croutons. Toss again. Make sure the salad plates are well chilled—grate some black pepper on top of them before serving the salad.

Coleslaw

This makes a large quantity but it keeps very well—up to two weeks in the refrigerator.

¾ cup vinegar
¾ cup sugar
¾ cup salad oil
1 tablespoon salt
1 teaspoon celery seed
1 large head cabbage, shredded
2 large carrots, grated
1 small onion, cut finely

Bring the vinegar, sugar, oil, salt, and celery seed to a boil. Pour this over the cabbage, carrots, and onion. Toss well and store in a covered container in the refrigerator.

Creamy Coleslaw

This has a lovely fresh cucumber flavor. Don't have too big an onion or it will overpower the cucumber.

1 cup sour cream
¼ cup mayonnaise
1 teaspoon celery seed
½ teaspoon dry mustard
juice of ½ lemon
1 teaspoon red wine vinegar

3 tablespoons sugar
1 medium to large head of cabbage, shredded
1 cucumber, peeled, finely grated
1 small onion, finely grated
1 cup chopped parsley
salt and pepper to taste

Mix the sour cream, mayonnaise, celery seed, dry mustard, lemon juice, wine vinegar, and sugar. Into a large bowl put the shredded cabbage, grated cucumber, grated onion, and chopped parsley. Pour the sauce over and mix well. Add salt and pepper to taste.

Cucumber Salad

This salad goes very nicely with fish—particularly salmon.

2 large cucumbers
1 cup mayonnaise
2 tablespoons grated onion
salt

Peel the cucumbers and slice thinly. Mix into the mayonnaise the grated onion. Arrange a layer of cucumbers in a shallow bowl and sprinkle with salt. Spread with a very thin layer of the mayonnaise mixture. Continue in this manner until all the cucumber is used up, ending with a layer of mayonnaise. Let stand in the refrigerator overnight.

Gazpacho Salad

A small glass punch bowl is perfect for this.

2 medium cucumbers, thinly sliced
1 teaspoon salt
⅔ cup salad oil
⅓ cup red wine vinegar
1 clove garlic, minced
1 teaspoon salt
1 teaspoon basil
½ teaspoon black pepper
½ pound mushrooms, sliced
4 green onions including tops, thinly sliced
1 small head cauliflower, separated into individual flowerets
3 large tomatoes, cut into wedges
½ cup minced parsley
1 large green pepper, seeded, thinly sliced

Put the cucumber slices into a bowl and sprinkle with 1 teaspoon of salt. Let stand for 30 minutes. Drain and pat dry. In a large salad bowl, preferably glass, combine the oil, vinegar, garlic, salt, basil, and pepper. Add the mushrooms, green onions, cauliflower, and cucumber slices. Mix gently. Add a layer of tomatoes, sprinkle with the chopped parsley, and top with the green pepper. Cover the bowl and chill for 4 hours. Just before serving, toss again. Serves 8.

Horseradish Mold

A very attractive and slightly different way of serving horseradish. Serve it with anything with which you enjoy horseradish. I stick mostly to beef dishes and assorted cold cuts, but I have seen horseradish served with fish as well. Be sure to tell your guests that this is a condiment, not a salad.

1 package celery flavored jello
1 cup boiling water
1 cup horseradish
1 cup heavy cream, whipped

Dissolve the jello in boiling water. When cool add the horseradish. When cold and just before it starts to congeal, fold in the whipped cream.

Marge's Carrot Salad

This is a great salad to serve at a buffet. It doubles beautifully and you can make it ahead of time.

2 pounds frozen baby carrots
1 large onion, sliced thinly into rings
1 large green pepper, sliced thinly
   into rings
¾ cup sugar
½ cup salad oil
1 teaspoon dry mustard

1 teaspoon Worcestershire sauce
½ teaspoon salt
¼ teaspoon pepper
¾ cup vinegar
1 can tomato soup

Cook the carrots and drain. When cool, put into a large salad bowl and arrange the onion rings and green pepper rings on top. Blend all the other ingredients together until the sugar is dissolved, then pour over the carrots, onions, and pepper. Let stand several hours or overnight. Serves 12.

Marinated Artichoke Hearts

1 egg yolk
½ cup olive oil
¼ cup wine vinegar
2 tablespoons Dijon mustard
2 tablespoons minced parsley
2 tablespoons chopped chives
1 tablespoon minced shallots
2 cans artichoke hearts (Tosca brand)

Mix together the egg yolk, olive oil, vinegar, mustard, parsley, chives, and shallots. Pour over the drained artichoke hearts. Let marinate overnight.

Orange and Onion Salad

Sound like a funny combination? Wait until you try it.

½ large mild onion
1 large orange
1 medium sized head romaine lettuce
½ teaspoon salt
½ teaspoon freshly ground black
  pepper

⅓ cup salad oil (scant)
2 tablespoons fresh lemon juice
1 tablespoon fresh orange juice
½ teaspoon sugar
½ teaspoon poppy seeds

Slice the onion and orange very thinly. Separate the onion into rings and be sure to remove all the white membrane from the orange. Tear the lettuce and arrange the sliced orange and onion rings on top. Mix the other ingredients in a small jar. Just before serving, shake well and pour over the salad. Toss and serve. Serves 6.

Peachy Ginger Salad Mold

Just a little different. Perfect with ham and a very attractive addition to any buffet table.

1 can peach halves
¼ teaspoon ground ginger
boiling water
2 packages orange jello, 3 ounce size
5 ounces pineapple cream cheese
¼ cup chopped pecans

Drain the syrup from the peaches and add the ginger. Add enough boiling water to the syrup to make 3 cups of liquid. Add the jello and dissolve. Pour enough of the jello into a 9 inch ring mold to fill it to a depth of 1 inch. Chill until firm. Meanwhile make 8 small cream cheese balls and roll them in the chopped nuts. Place the cheese balls over the chilled jello, spacing them evenly. Cover each ball with a peach half, round side up. Carefully pour the remaining unset jello mixture over the peaches. Chill until firm. Serves 8.

Thousand Island Ring

I was served this recently at a luncheon and thought it was excellent. The hostess very kindly supplied me with the recipe. The center is filled with seafood. I have since made it and it is very easy to put together.

2 tablespoons gelatin
½ cup cold water
1 cup chili sauce
1½ cups mayonnaise
6 hard-boiled eggs, chopped
1 cup celery, chopped
1 can pimento, diced
½ teaspoon sugar
dash of Tabasco sauce
1 teaspoon Worcestershire sauce
½ cup ketchup
(crab, shrimp, or lobster for center of ring)

Soak the gelatin in water to soften it, then place the dish over hot water to dissolve it. Mix together the remaining ingredients (except the seafood). Pour into a lightly oiled ring mold and chill until firm. Unmold. Fill the center with shrimp, crab, or lobster. Serves 8 to 10.

Tomato Aspic

Serve this with anything as it adapts itself easily to fish, fowl, or vegetables. Serve it with mayonnaise or any mayonnaise-based dressing.

4 cups tomato juice
3 tablespoons gelatin
salt and pepper to taste
1 teaspoon Worcestershire sauce
1 cup chopped green onion
1 tablespoon very finely chopped parsley
½ cup mayonnaise

Soak the gelatin in ½ cup cold tomato juice for 5 minutes. Heat the remaining 3½ cups of tomato juice, then dissolve the gelatin in it. Add the salt, pepper, and Worcestershire sauce. When cool, add the chopped green onions, parsley, and mayonnaise. Mold and chill.

Tomato Gelatin Salad

Prepare this salad 24 hours in advance.

1 can tomato soup
1 large package cream cheese
2 envelopes plain gelatin dissolved
   in ½ cup cold water
1 cup mayonnaise
1 cup chopped celery
½ cup chopped green pepper
1 small onion, grated
1 small bottle chopped stuffed olives, drained
1 teaspoon salt
dash of Worcestershire sauce

Bring the soup (undiluted) to a boil. Add the cream cheese and beat until smooth. Add the gelatin while this mixture is still warm. Add the remaining ingredients and pour into a mold or loaf pan. Chill overnight.

West Coast Onions

Super for a buffet. Great with roast beef.

3 Spanish onions
1 cup vinegar
½ cup white sugar
½ cup mayonnaise
1 teaspoon celery seed

Slice the onions thinly. Mix the vinegar and sugar until the sugar is dissolved. Pour this mixture over the onions and leave overnight. The next day, drain it very well. Mix the mayonnaise and celery seed and toss with the onions. Chill before serving. Serves 10 to 12.

ONE - I RELIEVE MY FRUSTRATIONS
TWO - I GET TO MAKE A GREAT WIENER SCHNITZEL !!

Salad Dressings

Aunt Helen's Salad Dressing

1 can condensed tomato soup
¾ cup vinegar
1 teaspoon salt
½ teaspoon pepper
½ teaspoon paprika
1 tablespoon Worcestershire sauce

⅓ to ½ cup granulated sugar
1 teaspoon minced onion
1 teaspoon prepared mustard
1½ cups salad oil
1 clove garlic, minced

Mix the ingredients in a blender, a little at a time. Store in the refrigerator.

Creamy Anchovy Garlic Dressing

Most gals know about the dressing made with buttermilk, mayonnaise, and Hidden Valley salad dressing mix, and how good it is on baked potatoes. Unfortunately we can't buy Hidden Valley mix in Canada anymore but you can substitute Great Beginnings avocado salad dressing mix and get equally good results. When I want something a little different to serve on romaine lettuce, I make the following.

2 cups mayonnaise
2 cups buttermilk
1 package Ranch Valley dressing mix (or Great Beginnings avocado mix)
½ tin anchovies (well drained)
2 cloves garlic, minced

Put all the ingredients into a blender and blend well.

Guacamole Salad Dressing

2 ripe avocados
1 tablespoon minced green onion, white part only
1 clove garlic, minced
¼ teaspoon chili powder
¼ teaspoon salt
dash white pepper
1 cup mayonnaise, thinned with a little cream
6 slices crisp bacon, crumbled

Mash the avocados and mix with all the other ingredients except the bacon. The bacon does not go into the dressing, but have it on hand to sprinkle over the salad.

The House Salad Dressing

I changed dressings many times before I finally settled on this one. I always keep a bottle on hand.

1 cup salad oil
¼ cup red wine vinegar
1 teaspoon salt
1 teaspoon freshly ground black pepper
1 teaspoon prepared mustard
1 teaspoon Worcestershire sauce

½ teaspoon dried basil
½ teaspoon minced garlic
1 tablespoon Parmesan cheese, grated
1 egg yolk
¼ teaspoon sugar (optional)

Put all the ingredients into a jar and shake well just before using.

Lynn's Green Onion Dressing

My daughter Lynn tasted a green goddess dressing which she thought was super. So she decided to try to duplicate it. This is what she came up with, thinking it might be just a wee bit better. Knowing Lynn's ingenuity in the kitchen, she is probably right. (You must have a blender to make this recipe.)

1 egg
1 teaspoon salt
1 teaspoon sugar
1 teaspoon dry mustard
pinch of cayenne pepper
3 tablespoons vinegar
1¼ cups oil

5 anchovies
⅓ cup parsley, packed
6 green onions, tops only
2 tablespoons sherry
¼ teaspoon freshly ground black
   pepper

Into the container of a blender put the egg, salt, sugar, mustard, cayenne pepper, and vinegar. Turn on the switch for just a few seconds. Take off the cover and add the oil very gradually until thick. Turn off the blender. Add the anchovies, parsley, green onion tops, sherry, and pepper. Blend again until well mixed. If dressing is too thick, thin it with a little cream, although this is usually unnecessary.

Roquefort Salad Dressing

1½ cups mayonnaise
2 tablespoons light cream
½ cup crumbled Roquefort cheese (or blue cheese)
1 teaspoon Worcestershire sauce
¼ teaspoon salt
⅛ teaspoon garlic powder
⅛ teaspoon white pepper

Mix all the ingredients together. Do not use a blender, as nice little pieces of the cheese should be identifiable.

Sesame Seed Dressing

1½ tablespoons sesame seeds, lightly toasted
½ cup salad oil
¼ cup soy sauce
2 tablespoons lemon juice
1½ tablespoons grated onion
½ teaspoon sugar
½ teaspoon pepper

Mix all the ingredients together. Let the mixture stand for 1 hour. This is too much dressing to use for ½ pound of spinach—judge how much is needed according to personal preference.

Sauces

SAVORY SAUCES
Blender Béarnaise Sauce

2 tablespoons white wine
1 tablespoon tarragon vinegar
2 teaspoons finely chopped shallots
  or onion
1 teaspoon tarragon
¼ teaspoon black pepper

½ cup butter
3 egg yolks
2 tablespoons lemon juice
¼ teaspoon salt
pinch of cayenne

Combine the first five ingredients in a saucepan and cook over high heat until almost all the liquid has evaporated. Set this mixture aside. Into the container of a blender put the egg yolks, lemon juice, salt, and cayenne. In a small saucepan heat to bubbling the ½ cup butter, but do not let it brown. As soon as the butter bubbles, remove the blender cover, and with the blender on low speed, add the hot butter in a steady stream. When all the butter is added, turn the motor off. Add the ingredients that have been previously reduced over high heat. Blend at high speed for about 4 seconds.

Blender Hollandaise Sauce

½ cup butter
3 egg yolks
2 tablespoons lemon juice (scant unless you like it fairly lemony)
¼ teaspoon salt
pinch of cayenne

Into the container of a blender put the egg yolks, lemon juice, salt, and cayenne. In a small saucepan heat to bubbling, but do not let brown, the ½ cup butter. As soon as the butter bubbles, quickly remove the cover of the blender and with the blender on low speed, add the hot butter in a steady stream. When all the butter is added, turn off the motor. Makes ¾ cup.

Caper Sauce

1 cup mayonnaise
¼ cup chopped capers
¼ cup fresh lemon juice
1 tablespoon caper juice

Combine all the ingredients. Heat them to serve with hot salmon, or chill for cold salmon.

Peter's Caper Sauce for Salmon Steaks

I like this on cold salmon as well.

¼ cup butter
1 tablespoon lemon juice (or to taste)
1 tablespoon chopped parsley
1 tablespoon capers
freshly ground pepper to taste

Brown the butter slightly. Immediately add the lemon juice, parsley, capers, and pepper. Bring to a boil and pour over broiled salmon steaks. (Don't use frozen salmon steaks—they lose their texture when frozen.)

Caviar Mayonnaise

This recipe is for that very special dinner party. Serve it with hot or cold salmon.

1 tablespoon tomato sauce
2 cups mayonnaise (I use Kraft, but if you have homemade on hand use it)
4 ounces red caviar

Stir the tomato sauce into the mayonnaise. Fold in the caviar very carefully. Chill.

Cheese Sauce

A recipe couldn't be easier than this. Great on cauliflower and broccoli, I also use it as the base for macaroni and cheese. Just make sure you have enough sauce for the amount of macaroni served.

1 can cheese soup
½ cup grated sharp Cheddar cheese

Combine the ingredients in a small saucepan and heat until the cheese is melted.

Cucumber Sauce

Nice with cold salmon and hot or cold tongue.

1 cucumber
¾ cup sour cream
¼ teaspoon salt
⅛ teaspoon paprika
2 teaspoons finely chopped chives

Pare, seed, and cut the cucumber finely. Drain well. Combine the sour cream, salt, paprika, and chives, then add the drained cucumber.

Cumberland Sauce

1 cup port wine
1 tablespoon cornstarch
1 cup red currant jelly
1 teaspoon prepared mustard
¼ teaspoon grated orange rind

Mix the cornstarch and wine. Add the remaining ingredients. Bring to a boil and simmer slowly until clear.

Egg Sauce for Poached or Whole Baked Salmon

Serve this or Caper Sauce (see index) with hot salmon. If you are entertaining anyone from the Maritime Provinces, be sure to serve the Egg Sauce!

1 cup mayonnaise
⅓ cup light cream (or thin to desired consistency)
2 hard-boiled eggs
salt and pepper to taste

Thin the mayonnaise with the cream. Add the sliced hard-boiled eggs and salt and pepper. Heat and serve.

Red Wine Sauce for Duck or Goose

This is the sauce I most frequently use for duck or goose, but I have also used Cumberland Sauce (see index) which is equally good.

½ cup red currant jelly (or plum jelly)
¼ cup red wine
¼ cup ketchup
½ teaspoon Worcestershire sauce
2 tablespoons butter

Combine all the ingredients in a saucepan and melt over low heat. Serve hot.

Sweet Mustard Sauce

Nice with boiled ham or for dipping meat balls when serving them as an hors d'oeuvre.

2 eggs
1 cup white sugar
⅔ cup white vinegar
4 tablespoons dry mustard

Beat the eggs well. Add all the other ingredients. Cook in a double boiler until thick. Store in the refrigerator.

SWEET SAUCES

Butter Sauce

Delicious over steamed puddings.

½ cup melted butter
¾ cup icing sugar
1 beaten egg

Cook in a double boiler until syrupy. This makes a rather small quantity. If serving more than six people, double the recipe.

Butterscotch Sauce

2 cups brown sugar
3/4 cup cream
butter the size of an egg

Boil about 20 minutes or until it thickens.

Chocolate Sauce

2½ squares bitter chocolate
1 cup icing sugar
½ cup evaporated milk (remaining milk can be used in reheating)
1 egg yolk
1 teaspoon salt
1 tablespoon butter
½ teaspoon vanilla

Melt the chocolate over low heat or in the top of a double boiler. Add half the sugar. Add the milk and mix well. Add the rest of the sugar, the egg yolk, and salt. Cook about 10 minutes until smooth and creamy. Stir occasionally. Add the butter and vanilla. Serve hot. When reheating, add more evaporated milk.

Melba Sauce

Peach Melba, a dessert I am sure you have seen on many menus, is simply a scoop of vanilla ice cream placed in the center of a peach half and covered with Melba Sauce.

1 cup crushed raspberries
1 cup red currant jelly
¼ cup water
½ cup sugar
1 teaspoon cornstarch

Mix together all the ingredients and cook over low heat until clear, about 10 minutes. Strain through a fine sieve and cool.

Seafood

Baked Whole Salmon

whole salmon
salt and freshly ground pepper (sea salt if available)
butter
thinly sliced lemon
thinly sliced tomato
oil

Always cook fish with the head and tail intact as this helps retain the juices. Season the fish inside and out with salt and pepper. Coat inside the fish with butter, also laying overlapping slices of very thinly sliced lemon and tomato along the inside. Enclose the fish securely with a large piece of well-oiled aluminum foil. Place it on a trivet in a large baking pan and put a bit of hot water in the bottom of the pan. This will help keep the fish moist. Another thing that helps to keep fish nice and moist is not over cooking it: bake for 1¼ to 1½ hours in a 325° oven (depending on the size of the fish—this timing was based on a 10 pound salmon). Check in 1¼ hours—just open the foil and test the thickest part of the fish with two forks, easing it apart slightly. If not cooked, return the salmon to the oven and continue cooking until it flakes easily when tested with a fork. As it is rather difficult to remove the fish from the foil, try poking a few holes in the bottom of the foil to drain excess juices, then turn the fish over very carefully onto a platter—or just fold the foil back very neatly and garnish with lots of parsley.

Salmon Cooked In Dishwasher:

If the fish is too long to fit into any baking pans, don't cut the fish in half—cook it in a dishwasher. First of all, run the empty dishwasher through a short cycle to remove any soapy residue and to clean the appliance thoroughly before placing the fish inside. Place the fish on two thicknesses of heavy-duty foil, large enough to double fold on all sides. Season the fish as in the preceding recipe. Carefully fold the foil loosely, leaving some air space (making sure it is double folded and double sealed so it will be watertight as well as airtight). Seal with masking tape to prevent the force of water from opening it. Place the fish on the top rack of the dishwasher, folding over any plate or cup holders and making sure no wires can puncture the foil. Run the fish through a full cycle. Make sure nobody has a shower or bath just before you cook the fish, as it is essential that the water be very hot! Check the fish for doneness by opening the foil slightly. If the fish flakes easily and tastes done, it is ready. If not, reseal the foil completely, using fresh masking tape if necessary to prevent water seepage, and reset the dishwasher to rinse cycle. (When cooking a 7 pound Arctic char, it took two complete cycles.) When the fish is ready, carefully transfer it to a platter long enough to hold the fish without bending or breaking it—a long wooden tray covered with foil might be the solution if the right sized platter is not available. Decorate the fish with fresh overlapping slices of lemon and sprigs of parsley.

Crabmeat en Ramekin

1 pound crabmeat
6 strips cooked bacon
¾ teaspoon dry mustard
½ teaspoon celery salt
½ teaspoon paprika
½ cup chili sauce
1 teaspoon white wine vinegar
1½ cups mayonnaise

Divide the crabmeat equally among 6 individual ramekin dishes. Heat in a 350° oven for 5 minutes. Top with bacon strips. Blend together the mustard, celery salt, paprika, chili sauce, and mayonnaise. Spread over the crab and bacon and place under the broiler until glazed. Serves 6.

Overnight Crab Soufflé

One of the nice features about this delicious crab soufflé is that you make it the day before—all but the cooking that is. Make sure your baking dish is large enough so that your soufflé doesn't spill over when it's baked. This recipe is perfect for a luncheon or light supper.

butter
2 tins crabmeat
½ cup mayonnaise
1 cup celery, minced
½ cup green pepper, chopped
½ cup green onion, chopped

8 slices white bread (day old)
4 eggs, large size
3 cups milk
1 tin cream of mushroom soup
1 cup grated Cheddar cheese

Butter a large casserole. (Make sure the casserole is large enough so that the soufflé will not spill over.) Mix the crabmeat, mayonnaise, celery, green pepper, and green onion. Remove the crusts from the bread and cut 4 of the slices into cubes. Arrange these cubes in the bottom of the casserole and top with the crabmeat mixture. Lay the remaining 4 slices of bread on top. Beat the eggs slightly and mix with the milk. Pour this over the mixture in the casserole and refrigerate overnight. The next day, bake in a 350° oven for 20 minutes. (Put the casserole into a pan of hot water for baking, if desired.) Remove and spread with the mushroom soup. Sprinkle with the grated cheese and return the casserole to the oven for 1 hour. Serves 8.

Scallops in Wine Sauce

This recipe for these delicious little shellfish was given to me shortly after I was married. I don't have many recipes for scallops because I like this one so much, I have not experimented further. I either bread and fry them or prepare them in the following manner.

2 pounds scallops	2 tablespoons parsley, minced
2 cups white wine	2 tablespoons flour
4 tablespoons butter	2 tablespoons cream, heavy
24 mushrooms, sliced	½ cup dry bread crumbs
4 green onions, finely chopped	2 tablespoons grated Swiss cheese

Wash the scallops and simmer in the 2 cups of white wine for about 6 minutes or until they are tender. Drain, reserving the wine. Sauté the mushrooms and onions in the butter. Add the parsley and blend in the flour. Add the reserved wine very slowly while stirring constantly. Stir in the cream. Combine the scallops with the sauce in a baking dish. Mix the dry bread crumbs with the grated cheese. Sprinkle over the scallops. Dot with a bit of butter and brown under the broiler. Serves 6 to 8.

Seafood Casserole

½ cup butter	2 tins lobster (5 ounce cans), drained
1 pound medium shrimp	3 tablespoons flour
⅓ cup chopped green onions	¼ cup sherry
⅓ cup chopped celery	2 cups milk
¼ cup chopped green pepper	¼ cup grated Cheddar cheese
¼ teaspoon salt	⅛ teaspoon cayenne pepper
⅛ teaspoon pepper	

Sauté the shrimp, onions, celery, green pepper, salt, and pepper in ¼ cup butter until the shrimp is done (about 5 minutes). Add the canned lobster. Sprinkle with flour. Reduce the heat and stir until the flour is absorbed. Add the sherry, stirring to mix. Add the milk and stir until the sauce thickens. (Add an additional small amount of milk if the sauce is too thick). Add the Cheddar cheese and cayenne. This can be served immediately with rice or in pastry shells, or it can be refrigerated at this point and reheated in a double boiler the next day. Alternately, it can be put into a casserole and refrigerated. The next day, top with buttered bread crumbs mixed with a little grated Cheddar cheese, and bake in a 350° oven for about ½ hour or until bubbly and the top is golden. This recipe is also delicious (and more economical) when you substitute 2 or 3 cans of tuna for the shrimp and lobster. Serves 6.

Seafood Mornay

This really is a simple dish. You can make the sauce in the morning and stop at the fish market on the way home from the golf course to pick up some nice freshly cooked crab or shrimp. Put them together and heat just before you want to serve dinner. Some rice or boiled and buttered shell macaroni plus a nice spinach salad would complete the meal.

Line a shallow casserole with any cooked seafood (about 2 cups). Cover with the following sauce.

Mornay Sauce:

5 tablespoons butter   ½ cup grated sharp cheese
3 tablespoons flour   pepper to taste
½ teaspoon salt   3 dashes Tabasco sauce
1 cup milk   dash of garlic powder
½ cup white wine   2 egg yolks

Melt the butter. Blend in the flour and salt. Add the milk, wine, and cheese. Cook until this mixture thickens. Remove it from the heat, and add the garlic powder, Tabasco sauce, and egg yolks. Add pepper to taste. (Remember to add a little of the hot mixture to the egg yolks first). Beat well and pour over the seafood. Serves 4.

Shellfish Casserole

2 cans large shrimp
1 can lobster (tails are usable)
1 can crabmeat
⅓ cup butter
2 cups sliced fresh mushrooms
¼ cup chopped green onions
⅓ cup flour

½ teaspoon salt
1¾ cups milk
1 cup light cream
2 tablespoons sherry
1 cup crushed crisp rice cereal
2 tablespoons melted butter

Preheat the oven to 375°. Drain, rinse, and de-vein the shrimp. Drain and break up the lobster. Drain and flake the crabmeat. Melt the butter in a large saucepan. Sauté the mushrooms and onions until they are just tender. Blend in the flour and salt. Remove from the heat and gradually stir in the milk and cream. Cook over medium heat, stirring constantly until thickened. Stir in the shrimp, lobster, crab, and sherry. Turn into a 2 quart casserole. Combine the crushed cereal and melted butter. Sprinkle it over the casserole. Bake in a 350° oven until the topping is crisp and golden, about 30 minutes. Serves 8.

Shrimp Lucie

Shrimp Lucie should really be Shrimp Mary because that is the name of the woman who gave me the recipe—but only after I promised in return to give her my recipe for Almond Crisps AND show her how to make it. It was a fair trade!

6 tablespoons butter
4 green onions
1 large clove garlic
1 green pepper
½ cup tomato sauce
1 tablespoon Worcestershire sauce
salt and freshly ground pepper
¾ cup béchamel sauce (medium white sauce)
2 cups cooked shrimp

Melt the butter in a skillet. Chop the green onions and garlic very finely. Chop the green pepper. Add the chopped vegetables to the melted butter and simmer gently until tender, making sure they do not brown. Add the tomato sauce, Worcestershire sauce, salt, and pepper, and continue simmering for 5 minutes. Slowly add the béchamel sauce and correct the seasoning if necessary. Place the shrimp into this sauce and simmer until heated throughout. Serve with rice. Serves 4.

Seka's Sole

Like the woman who gave me this recipe—it is very elegant.

3 pounds fillet of sole	4 tablespoons butter
¾ pound mushrooms	3 to 4 tablespoons flour
4 green onions, chopped	¾ cup whipping cream
2 tablespoons butter	½ teaspoon salt or to taste
1 cup dry vermouth	pepper to taste

Wash and drain the fish. Pat dry and cut into serving pieces of uniform size. Melt the 2 tablespoons of butter in a skillet and sauté the mushrooms and onions very lightly. Butter a shallow flameproof baking dish, large enough to hold the fillets in one layer. Lay the fillets side by side, folding them in half if they are less than ¼ inch thick. Salt and pepper the fish and spread with the mushrooms and onions. Pour the vermouth over the fish carefully and add enough water to barely cover it. Bring close to simmering on top of the stove, then transfer to a pre-heated 350° oven and bake 8 to 10 minutes or until the fillets are just firm to the touch. Drain all juice into a saucepan. Boil this poaching liquid until it is reduced to 1 cup. Meanwhile, melt the 4 tablespoons of butter and stir in the flour. Add the reduced liquid slowly. Add the cream, salt, and pepper. Pour this sauce over the fish and place it under the broiler until the surface starts to brown. Serves 6 to 8.

Sole and Crab in Silver Triangles

1 cup sour cream	1 tablespoon lemon juice
2 tablespoons chopped green onion	¼ teaspoon salt
2 tablespoons chopped green pepper	dash of pepper
2 tablespoons sweet pickle relish	1 pound sole fillets
1 tablespoon chopped parsley	1 can crab, drained

Mix together all the ingredients except the fillets and crab—this is the sauce. Drain the fillets. Dry them well with paper towels. Cut four 12 inch squares of foil, crease them diagonally then unfold. For each package, place a portion of the sole on one side of the crease. Place ¼ can of crab on top of the sole and spoon ¼ of the sauce on top of the crab. Lift the lower edges of the foil upward slightly and fold the top over, sealing securely. Place the packages into a baking dish and bake in a 350° oven for 20 minutes. Just before serving, prick the bottom of the packages to release excess juices. These foil packages can be made in the morning and put into the refrigerator until ready to bake later in the day. Serve with spinach and rice. Serves 4.

Sole with Parsley Butter Sauce

This is a simple and delicious recipe, but please don't over cook the fish. Don't over cook ANY fish!

1 pound sole fillets
slightly beaten egg
dry pancake mix

Dip the pieces of sole in beaten egg then shake in a bag containing the pancake mix to coat the fish. Sauté in butter until golden, about 3 minutes on each side. Transfer to a heated serving platter while making the sauce.

Parsley Butter Sauce:

2 tablespoons green onions, chopped
¼ cup butter
2 tablespoons minced parsley
¼ cup red wine vinegar

Sauté the green onions in the ¼ cup butter. Add the parsley. When the butter starts to turn light brown, add the ¼ cup wine vinegar. Bring to a boil, stirring constantly, and pour over the fish. Serves 4.

Meat

Chinese Beef and Greens

1½ pound sirloin steak, cut into narrow strips
seasoned flour (to ¼ cup flour, add ¼ teaspoon salt, ¼ teaspoon black pepper, ⅛ teaspoon paprika)
1 clove garlic, minced
3 tablespoons oil
1 cup water
1 basket fresh mushrooms, sliced (or substitute canned)
3 tablespoons soy sauce
1 onion, cut into four, then thinly sliced lengthwise
1 green pepper, sliced
1 cup celery, sliced on the bias
½ Chinese cabbage (bok choy), shredded
1 head broccoli, the top separated into small flowerets, the stem pared and sliced on the bias
salt and pepper to taste

Shake the meat in the seasoned flour (in a paper bag) and brown it with the garlic in 2 or 3 tablespoons of oil. Add ½ cup water, the mushrooms, and soy sauce. Let simmer about 5 minutes. Add all the other vegetables and the remaining ½ cup water and simmer for 5 more minutes (the vegetables should be a bit crisp). Check the seasoning—since the soy sauce is salty, not too much salt is required. If there is too much liquid in the pan, thicken it with a bit of cornstarch. Serves 4 to 6.

Chuck Roast for Barbecuing

This makes a relatively inexpensive barbecue. The meat is delicious and makes great sandwiches the next day, IF there is any left!

1 chuck roast
½ cup soy sauce
⅔ cup sauterne
½ onion, finely minced

Slice the roast in half lengthwise and sprinkle with tenderizer (non-seasoned). Let stand overnight in the refrigerator. The next day, mix the soy sauce, wine, and minced onion. Marinate the meat all day in this sauce. Use the sauce for basting.

Leftover Roast Beef Casserole

Highly nutritious and easily prepared.

3 to 4 cups leftover roast beef, cut into cubes
1 can tomatoes, 14 ounce size
1 package Lipton onion soup mix
1 small can baked beans (smallest size)
1 small can tomato sauce
garlic salt to taste
¼ teaspoon oregano
onions and carrots, cut up

Mix all the ingredients together and bake, covered, in a 350° oven for 1 hour. If the casserole is a little too liquid, stir and bake for an additional ½ hour, uncovered.

Pot Roast

Most people enjoy a good pot roast. These are two very simple but tasty ways to prepare it.

#1

3½ to 4 pound boneless chuck roast
½ package dehydrated onion soup mix
1 can cream of mushroom soup

Wipe the meat with a damp cloth. Sprinkle the dry soup mix on both sides of the meat. Place into a shallow pan. Pour the undiluted mushroom soup over the meat. Cover with foil and bake for 3 hours in a 325° oven or until tender.

#2

Sprinkle the roast with garlic salt. Brown on both sides under the broiler. Reduce the heat to 325°. Cover the roasting pan and bake until tender, about 3 hours. One hour before the meat is done, add 1 package of Lipton's onion soup mix. Vegetables can be added at this time—for example, small whole onions, carrots, and potatoes. But any other vegetables would be as good, according to preference. The juice from the meat combined with the onion soup flavor gives them a super flavor.

Steak Diane

At least this is my version!

2 tablespoons butter	½ cup dry vermouth
2 tablespoons oil	1 tablespoon Dijon mustard
4 tenderloin steaks, or rib eye steaks	2 teaspoons Worcestershire sauce
½ cup chopped green onions	2 tablespoons chopped parsley
½ cup chopped mushrooms	salt and pepper to taste

In an electric frying pan melt the butter and mix with the oil. Brown the steaks quickly. When they are done, remove them to a warm platter. Add the chopped green onions and mushrooms to the pan and sauté until the onions are soft. Add the vermouth. Bring to a boil and cook for 2 minutes, stirring occasionally. Mix together the mustard, Worcestershire sauce, and parsley, and add to the pan. Return to boiling while stirring constantly. Pour this sauce over the steaks. Serves 4.

Beef Tenderloin Steak with Red Wine and Pimentos

So simple and so good!

4 tablespoons butter
1 tablespoon oil
4 individual tenderloin steaks
1 large onion, finely chopped
2 to 3 ounces pimentos, chopped
½ cup dry red wine
salt and freshly ground pepper to taste

Melt the 2 tablespoons of butter and mix with the 1 tablespoon of oil in a skillet. When hot, add the steaks and brown quickly. When cooked (try not to over cook) remove to a heated platter. Add the remaining 2 tablespoons of butter and the chopped onion to the skillet. Sauté until the onion is soft. Add the pimentos and cook for an additional minute or two. Add the wine and let it boil, stirring constantly. Boil for 1 minute on high heat. Add salt and pepper to taste. Spoon this sauce over the steaks. Serves 4.

Gracie's Friday Night Stir-Fry

This recipe comes from one of my favorite golfing buddies who is a good neighbor as well. If you have the ingredients on hand, it doesn't take long to prepare this tasty dish. If you are having friends in after a golf game, slice everything ahead and keep it in the refrigerator.

3 to 4 tablespoons butter
2 tenderloin steaks, 8 to 10 ounces each
1 large onion, thinly sliced
2 small green peppers, thinly sliced
1 clove garlic, minced
1 pound mushrooms, sliced
4 tomatoes, coarsely chopped
salt and freshly ground black pepper

Slice the steaks thinly, at an angle—this is easier to do if they are partially frozen. Melt the butter and sauté the beef quickly over high heat. Don't spoil the tenderloin by over cooking it. Put the beef aside on a heated platter. Begin stir-frying the rest of the vegetables beginning with the onions, green peppers, and garlic. When these have been cooking about 2 minutes, add the mushrooms and cook an additional 2 minutes. Now add the tomatoes, stirring constantly because they are going to produce a nice sauce. This will take only a minute or two. Return the meat and stir until nicely coated with this sauce. Correct the seasoning to taste. This recipe goes well served with rice and a tossed green salad. Serves 4.

Note: Shrimp may be substituted for the beef.

Delicious Beef Stew

You can put this stew into the oven and have enough time not only to play a game of golf, but also to stop at the bakery on the way home for some fresh crusty rolls to go with it.

flour and seasonings
2 pounds good stewing meat (not round steak, which tends to dry out)
1 onion, chopped
1 cup sliced carrots
8 ounces (canned) small whole onions, drained
2 cans golden mushroom soup
generous cup red wine
1 package dehydrated onion soup mix

Flour and season the beef. (Add ½ teaspoon salt and ¼ teaspoon black pepper to ¼ cup flour). Brown it well. Remove to a casserole. Brown the onion and add it to the meat in the casserole. Add the carrots and canned onions to the casserole. Combine the mushroom soup, red wine, and dehydrated onion soup mix. Pour over the meat and vegetables. Cover and cook slowly in a 275° oven for 5 to 6 hours. Serves 4 to 6.

COULD YOU DEMONSTRATE
THAT WILD THRASHING
MOVEMENT AGAIN? IT'S
JUST THE THING I NEED
TO MAKE A FINE
MERINGUE !!

Canneloni

I make this canneloni in stages so it doesn't seem like too big a job. I make the crêpes and the béchamel sauce the day before, the filling the next morning, and put the dish together one hour before baking time. This freezes beautifully and is very nice to have on hand for unexpected guests or for very busy days. Do not freeze the canneloni with the sauce. I freeze the filled crêpes on a cookie sheet, then transfer them into plastic bags for storage.

Crêpes:

2 cups flour
½ teaspoon salt
4 large eggs
1 cup cold water
1 cup cold milk
4 tablespoons butter, melted

Put all the ingredients into a blender and blend for 1 or 2 minutes—if no blender is available, use the following method. Sift the flour and salt into a bowl and make a well. Break the eggs into the well and beat lightly into the flour with a wire whisk, gradually adding the water and milk. Add the butter and set aside for 1 hour. To make the crêpes, use a 5 or 6 inch crêpe pan or a non-stick skillet. Heat it well then brush with oil. Lift the pan from the heat and pour in about 1½ tablespoons of the batter per crêpe, swirling the pan so that the batter covers the bottom thinly. Cook until set and the edge is dry—this should take 1 or 2 minutes. Lift carefully with a spatula and turn over gently, or grasp the crêpe with the fingers of both hands and turn to cook the other side for about 30 seconds. To store the crêpes, put waxed paper between each one, stack them and wrap the stack in foil. Store in the refrigerator or freezer.

Filling:

2 pounds fresh spinach
1 cup Ricotta cheese
¼ cup butter
¼ cup flour, sifted
½ cup milk
½ pound ground beef

3 ounces fresh mushrooms
¼ cup Parmesan cheese
½ cup minced onion, sautéed
⅛ teaspoon nutmeg
pinch of garlic powder
salt and pepper to taste

Cook the spinach until soft (not more than 5 minutes). Press into a colander to remove all excess moisture. Put through the finest blade of a food chopper, then mix with the Ricotta cheese. In a large skillet melt the butter and stir in the flour. Gradually add the milk and cook until smooth and thick. Put the ground beef and mushrooms through the finest blade of the food chopper. Mix well and add to the sauce in the skillet. Cook over medium heat, stirring until the beef is cooked and no pink remains. Cook 2 to 3 minutes longer, then add the Parmesan cheese, sautéed onion, nutmeg, garlic powder, salt, and pepper. Remove from the heat and allow to cool slightly. Stir into the spinach and cheese mixture. Adjust the seasonings and chill.

Tomato Sauce:

14 ounces Hunt's tomato sauce
7½ ounces Gattuso pizza sauce
¼ teaspoon oregano
¼ teaspoon basil

Mix the above ingredients together.

Béchamel Sauce:

¼ cup butter
¼ cup flour
2½ cups milk
½ teaspoon salt
⅛ teaspoon pepper
¼ cup grated Parmesan cheese

Melt the butter in a saucepan. Blend in the flour and gradually stir in the milk. Cook and stir until the sauce thickens and comes to a boil. Stir in the salt, pepper, and Parmesan cheese.

Mozzarella Cheese:

Have this on hand, grated.

TO ASSEMBLE THE CANNELONI:

Place 3 tablespoons of the filling on each crêpe and roll it up. Butter a large shallow baking dish, or individual dishes (2 canneloni per individual dish). Cover the bottom of the baking dish with ½ the tomato sauce. Lay the canneloni side by side over the sauce (do not layer). Cover with the rest of the tomato sauce then top with the béchamel sauce. Sprinkle with Mozzarella cheese. Bake in a 400° oven for 15 to 20 minutes, until heated throughout and the cheese is melted. Serves 10 to 12 (22 to 24 crêpes).

Chili Con Carne

This freezes well, so it can be made ahead of time for planned golf days.

2 pounds ground lean beef
1 cup chopped onion
¼ cup chopped green pepper
2 apples, sliced
1 teaspoon salt
3 cups tomato juice
½ cup chopped celery
2 tablespoons chili powder
2 cans kidney beans

Brown the meat in a Dutch oven. Add all the other ingredients except for the kidney beans and simmer for 1 hour. Add the kidney beans and simmer for an additional hour or until it reaches desired thickness. Serves 6 to 8.

Marion's Lasagna

This recipe is a little time consuming, but well worth the effort. You can start making it two days ahead of time, which spreads the work out and leaves you relatively free the day of the dinner. If you don't have a lasagna pan, you should buy one just for this recipe—you will want to use it again and again.

Sauce (make ahead):

2½ to 3 pounds ground round or good lean ground beef	1 teaspoon sweet basil
salt and pepper to taste	¼ teaspoon chili powder
1 teaspoon sugar	2 teaspoons oregano
1 cup chopped onion	2 teaspoons parsley flakes
2 cans tomatoes (20 ounce size)	2 stalks celery (whole)
2 cans tomato paste (5½ ounce size)	2 medium bay leaves
	4 whole cloves

Brown the meat with the salt, pepper, sugar, and onions. Put the tomatoes, tomato paste, basil, chili powder, oregano, and parsley into a blender and turn on for a few seconds (just enough to mash the tomatoes). Pour into a large saucepan and add the meat mixture, celery, bay leaves, and cloves (tie the bay leaves, celery, and cloves in a piece of gauze to make them easier to remove later). Simmer for ½ hour. Refrigerate for 24 hours.

To Assemble:

cooked lasagna noodles (use 15 narrow ones—5 per layer, or split 7½ regular
    ones, as they are easier to cut when eating, and easier on the waistline)
4 packages Mozzarella cheese (long package)—one package per layer is needed
grated Parmesan cheese

Remove the bay leaves, cloves, and celery from the meat sauce. Cover the bottom of a lasagna dish with some of the meat sauce, followed by a layer of cooked noodles, then a layer of Mozzarella cheese—sprinkle about 2 tablespoons of Parmesan cheese on top of the Mozzarella. Repeat these layers twice more, topping the third layer with meat sauce and arranging 6 squares of Mozzarella on top. Refrigerate until 1 hour before baking. If there is any remaining sauce, heat and serve it separately for those who would like extra. Bake in a 375° oven for about 1 hour (use foil to catch any drips). Cut into 12 portions immediately, then let stand for 15 minutes before serving to allow the lasagna to set.

Moussaka

This recipe comes from June Marshall, a fellow golfer. When part of my golf game breaks down (which seems to happen on a fairly regular basis), June is also my golf consultant. Although moussaka is traditionally made with ground lamb, June has substituted ground beef, as it is more readily available.

2 tablespoons butter	1 pound ground beef
2 tablespoons flour	15 ounces tomato sauce
½ teaspoon salt	1 teaspoon parsley flakes
¼ teaspoon pepper	1 teaspoon salt
1½ cups milk	½ teaspoon oregano
2 eggs	½ teaspoon cinnamon
2 onions, chopped	½ cup bread crumbs
1 clove garlic, minced	2 medium sized eggplants
⅓ cup vegetable oil	⅓ cup oil

Melt the butter and stir in the flour, salt, and pepper. Gradually stir in the milk. Cook, stirring constantly until the mixture thickens. Remove from the heat. Beat the eggs in a small bowl and stir in ¼ cup of the hot cream sauce. Add this to the remaining cream sauce and cook for an additional 1 minute. Remove from the heat and set aside. Sauté the onions and garlic until soft in ⅓ cup of oil in a large skillet. Add the meat and cook until brown. Drain off excess fat. Add the tomato sauce, parsley, salt, oregano, and cinnamon. Stir thoroughly. Cover and simmer for 30 minutes. Remove from the heat and add the bread crumbs. Cut the eggplants into ½ inch slices. Brush with the remaining ⅓ cup of oil. Place them on cookie sheets and broil 4 minutes on each side or until golden. Place ½ of the eggplant slices into the bottom of a large shallow greased baking dish. Spread the meat mixture evenly over top and cover with the remaining eggplant slices. Pour the cream sauce over top and bake for 1 hour in a 350° oven. Let stand 15 minutes before serving. Moussaka can be frozen or refrigerated before baking, but bring it to room temperature first. Serves 8.

Norwegian Meatballs

This recipe is wonderful party fare. Put the meatballs into a chafing dish and pass around with sweet mustard sauce (see page 58) for dipping. Any leftovers will freeze well. If it is for a large crowd (or a group of teenagers) you can double this recipe.

3 pounds ground beef
2 eggs
½ teaspoon nutmeg
½ teaspoon ginger
4 tablespoons flour
2 tablespoons cornstarch

2 medium onions, chopped finely
1½ teaspoons salt
dash of cayenne
1½ cups milk
20 crackers, finely crushed

Mix together all the ingredients. Form the mixture into balls and fry them until brown. Remove them from the pan and put into a casserole. Cover and bake in a 350° oven for 30 minutes.

Spaghetti Sauce

I think the two things with which we experiment most are salad dressings and spaghetti sauces. You would have to go a long way to find a better spaghetti sauce than this one.

1½ pounds ground beef
1 large onion, chopped
1 small green pepper, chopped
1 minced garlic bud, or to taste
2 tablespoons lemon juice
2 tablespoons Worcestershire sauce
1 cup ketchup

1 large can tomato soup
 (or two small cans)
1 can tomatoes, cut up (14 ounce size)
salt and pepper to taste
½ teaspoon oregano
½ pound sautéed mushrooms (optional)

Brown the meat and pour off any fat. Add all the other ingredients and simmer ½ hour, stirring frequently as this burns very easily on the bottom. This sauce keeps very well in the refrigerator and freezes well, too. It is a good idea to make double the recipe and freeze half for future use.

Zucchini Pie

We had an abundance of zucchini in the garden one year, so I tried several ways of presenting it to the family. This was one recipe they felt deserved repeating, so I made several of these pies for the freezer. They're very handy to have in reserve.

½ pound ground beef
2 tablespoons salad oil
½ cup chopped green pepper
½ teaspoon minced onion
1 teaspoon chopped parsley
1 teaspoon salt
1 teaspoon oregano
pastry for a 2 crust pie

3 medium sized zucchini
½ cup dry bread crumbs
½ cup grated Parmesan cheese
1 can whole tomatoes (14 ounce size)
milk
pepper
½ teaspoon garlic salt

Brown the meat in the salad oil. Add the green pepper, onion, parsley, salt, and oregano. Line a pie plate with one pastry. Slice ½ of the zucchini into this pastry-lined plate, and sprinkle with ½ the meat mixture and ½ the crumbs mixed with the cheese. Repeat. Arrange slices of the tomato on top. Cover with the second pastry, making a vent in the center. Brush the pastry with milk and sprinkle with pepper and garlic salt. Bake at 450° for 10 minutes, then reduce the heat to 350° and continue cooking until done—about 35 to 40 minutes. Serve hot. Serves 6.

Braised Lamb Shanks

This is one of those satisfying, hearty meals that requires no preliminary dish (like an appetizer or soup) before, and very little after.

6 lamb shanks
seasoned whole wheat flour
¼ cup shortening
2 tablespoons flour
1 clove garlic, minced

1 cup red wine
½ cup consommé
½ teaspoon crushed rosemary
2 tablespoons minced parsley

Shake the lamb in a bag containing the seasoned whole wheat flour. Brown it carefully in the shortening. Remove it to a large casserole. Sauté the garlic lightly in the pan in which the lamb shanks were browned, then add the 2 tablespoons of flour. Slowly add the wine and ½ cup of consommé. Cook and stir until the mixture starts to thicken. Pour it over the lamb shanks in the casserole. Sprinkle with the rosemary and parsley. Cover and bake in a 350° oven for 2 to 3 hours or until tender. Turn once or twice during cooking. Serves 6.

Roast Leg of New Zealand Lamb

*If you let the lamb thaw slowly in the refrigerator for two days and use the
following recipe, you would almost think you were eating Cape Breton spring
lamb, which is the finest lamb in the whole of Canada.*

⅓ cup vinegar
salt and pepper to taste
½ teaspoon paprika
½ teaspoon ginger
2 cloves garlic, minced
1 leg of lamb, thawed
¼ cup vinegar and ½ cup water mixed

Mix the ⅓ cup of vinegar with the salt, pepper, paprika, ginger, and garlic. Rub
the lamb well with this mixture and let it sit in the refrigerator overnight.
Preheat the oven to 450°. Place the lamb in the oven and immediately regulate
the temperature to 325°. Roast for 30 to 35 minutes per pound or until tender,
basting with the vinegar/water mixture.

Liver Chinese Style

*None of the children complain about having to eat liver when I prepare it this
way!*

1 pound calves' liver
cornstarch
5 tablespoons oil
4 green onions, white and green parts, sliced
3 tablespoons soy sauce
1 tablespoon sherry
1 teaspoon sugar
1 teaspoon salt

Cut the liver in ½ inch strips and dip into the cornstarch. Heat the oil in a skillet
and cook the liver for only 2 minutes on each side. Add the green onions and mix
with the liver. Combine the soy sauce, sherry, sugar, and salt, and pour over the
liver and onions. Mix thoroughly and cook for 1 minute. Serves 4.

Liver Patties

These are great to serve at a Sunday brunch. You can prepare the liver mixture the night before, then fry it just before serving.

3 slices bacon, cooked and crumbled
1 pound liver, ground
2 tablespoons onion, grated
½ teaspoon salt
dash of pepper
4 tablespoons flour
1 egg, beaten

Combine the bacon, liver, onion, salt, pepper, flour, and egg. The mixture will look a little runny but don't be concerned, it is supposed to. When ready to cook, drop by spoonfuls into a frying pan which has some bacon drippings (saved from cooking the bacon), or use melted butter. Cook, turning once, until the patties are browned on both sides. Serves 4.

Baked Deviled Pork Chops

Pour the delicious sauce from these pork chops over rice or mashed potatoes and serve with the meal.

8 pork chops, trimmed of excess fat
garlic salt
1 large onion, finely chopped
4 tablespoons lemon juice
1 cup ketchup
1 teaspoon dry mustard
2 tablespoons brown sugar
2 teaspoons Worcestershire sauce

Sprinkle the chops with the garlic salt and brown in a skillet. Transfer them to a large baking dish. Combine the onion, lemon juice, ketchup, mustard, brown sugar, and Worcestershire sauce. Spoon this mixture over the pork chops. Bake in a 325° oven for 1 hour. Serves 8.

Pork Pie (Tourtière)

When my husband and I were first married, we lived in a French-Canadian community where tourtière was a traditional New Year's Eve dish. I have tried several recipes given to me by friends from Bathurst, New Brunswick, a predominantly French community, and from Montreal. After trying several recipes, all of them good, I settled on this one which is a favorite of my husband's.

1 pound ground pork	¼ teaspoon allspice, scant
½ cup water	¼ teaspoon cloves, scant
¼ cup dry oatmeal	¾ teaspoon salt
1 medium onion, chopped	pastry for a 2 crust pie
1 clove garlic, finely minced	milk
¼ teaspoon thyme	pepper to taste
¼ teaspoon oregano	garlic salt

Mix together all the ingredients except the last four. Cook over low heat, stirring frequently for 1 hour. Let the mixture cool—this is the pie filling. Put it into a 9 inch pastry shell and cover with the top pastry. Brush the pastry with milk and sprinkle it with pepper and garlic salt. Bake in a 400° oven until the pastry is golden brown. Serves 6.

Pork Tenderloin with Orange Sauce

2 pounds pork tenderloin	2 tablespoons sugar
2 tablespoons butter	1 teaspoon salt, or to taste
2 tablespoons grated onion	dash of pepper
1 teaspoon grated orange rind	1 bay leaf
⅔ cup orange juice	1 tablespoon cornstarch
½ cup dry sherry	1 tablespoon cold water

Brown the meat on all sides. Remove the meat and in the same pan, sauté the onion in butter until soft. Add the orange rind and juice, sherry, sugar, salt, pepper, and bay leaf. Return the meat to the pan. Cover and simmer slowly for 1 hour or until tender, turning occasionally. Remove the meat to a hot platter. Combine the cornstarch and water to make a paste. Stir it into the orange mixture and bring to a boil. Cook and stir until clear, about 1 to 2 minutes. Slice the meat and pour the sauce over it. Serves 6.

Sherry Roast Pork Parkins

5 pounds rolled loin of pork
½ cup sherry
⅓ cup orange juice
1 teaspoon horseradish
½ cup brown sugar
2 teaspoons grated orange rind
1 teaspoon prepared mustard
parsley

Place the roast into a shallow pan—try a broiler pan lined with foil, which makes for easy cleaning. Bake for 1 hour in a 325° oven. In a saucepan combine the sherry, orange juice, horseradish, brown sugar, orange rind, and mustard, and bring to a boil. Pour this sauce over the pork and bake for 2 to 3 hours longer, basting frequently. Remove to a heated platter and decorate with parsley—a lovely contrast to the dark brown color.

Sausage Crêpes

These are perfect for a brunch or a luncheon, and they are SO good!

Crêpes:

2 cups flour
¼ teaspoon salt
4 large eggs
1 cup cold water
1 cup cold milk
4 tablespoons melted butter

Put all the ingredients into a blender, except the melted butter. Blend for 1 or 2 minutes. Add the melted butter and blend again for about 10 seconds. Set aside for 1 hour. If no blender is available, use the following method. Sift the flour and salt into a bowl and make a well. Break the eggs into the well and beat lightly into the flour with a wire whisk, gradually adding the water and milk. Mix in the melted butter and set aside for 1 hour. To make the crêpes, use a 5 or 6 inch crêpe pan or a non-stick skillet. (Make sure there are no scratches on the bottom of the skillet or the crêpes will stick.) Heat the pan well then brush with oil. Lift the pan from the heat and pour in just enough batter, about 1½ tablespoons, and swirl the pan so that the batter covers the bottom thinly. Cook until set and the edge starts to dry—this should take 30 to 40 seconds. Lift carefully with a spatula and turn over gently, or grasp the crêpe with the fingers of both hands and turn to cook the other side, which should take only about 20 to 30 seconds. To store the crêpes, put waxed paper between each one before stacking.

Filling:

1 pound mildly seasoned sausage meat
¼ cup chopped onion
3 ounces cream cheese, cubed
¼ teaspoon garlic salt
½ cup sour cream
1 can mushroom stems and pieces, drained (10 ounce size)
½ cup sharp Cheddar cheese, grated
chopped parsley

Sauté the sausage meat and onion until cooked, breaking the sausage meat up slightly as it cooks. Drain very well. Stir in the cream cheese, garlic salt, and sour cream until the cream cheese has melted. Stir in the mushroom pieces and grated Cheddar cheese. Remove from heat. If the mixture seems too thick at this point, add 1 or 2 tablespoons of milk. Let cool slightly. Place 2 tablespoons of filling on each crêpe and roll—there should be enough filling for 12 crêpes. (They may be frozen at this stage.) When ready to cook, allow to thaw first, then bake covered in a 350° oven for 20 to 30 minutes. Sprinkle the tops with chopped parsley. Serves 6.

Barbecued Spareribs

This recipe comes from a friend who has been playing golf for years, from a time when I thought of it as a really dumb game! Continued basting of the ribs will preserve them indefinitely—for those 'can't get it together on time' friends.

3 to 5 pounds ribs
½ cup molasses
½ cup ketchup
½ cup chopped onion
3 whole cloves
4 narrow strips orange rind, diced finely
1½ cups orange juice
1 tablespoon vinegar

1 tablespoon salad oil
½ teaspoon prepared mustard
¼ teaspoon salt
¼ teaspoon pepper
dash of Tabasco sauce
½ teaspoon Worcestershire sauce
1 tablespoon butter
1 tablespoon bottled barbecue sauce

Mix together all the ingredients except the ribs and simmer for 5 minutes. Trim the fat from the ribs and the skin from the back of them. Line a broiler pan with foil. Lay the strips of ribs with the curved or bone side down. Cover each layer of ribs with waxed paper and roast in a 325° oven for ½ hour. Pour off the excess fat. Roast for an additional ½ hour and again pour off the fat. (Put a broiler rack over the ribs and it will be easier to pour off the fat without the ribs landing in the sink!) Remove the waxed paper and cover the ribs with the sauce made earlier which has simmered for 5 minutes. Bake in a 325° oven for at least an additional 2 hours, basting with plain orange juice after the first hour. Nearly a whole can of frozen orange juice (36 ounces diluted) can be used for the sauce and the basting. Dinner can be delayed by repeated basting with this orange juice sauce.

Sweetbreads on Anchovy Toast

*This is my favorite way of preparing sweetbreads. I just wish I could find
fresh ones regularly. Do serve them on the anchovy toast. It is a wonderful
combination of flavors.*

1 pair sweetbreads
salt
lemon juice
flour
2 tablespoons butter
2 tablespoons chopped green onion
1 tablespoon chopped parsley
⅓ cup vermouth, more or less

Soak the sweetbreads in cold water for 1 hour, changing the water when it
becomes tinged with pink—several changes may be required. Drain. Put the
sweetbreads into a saucepan with cold salted water to which a bit of lemon juice
has been added. Bring slowly to a boil and simmer uncovered for about 15
minutes. Drain and plunge them into cold water to firm. When they have
cooled, drain again and trim by removing the cartilage, tubes, connective tissue,
and tougher membrane. Cut into slices but not too thinly. Dip the slices into
flour and sauté in the butter until nicely golden on both sides. Remove the
sweetbreads to a heated platter and keep warm. Sauté the onion and parsley in
the same skillet—another tablespoon of butter may be needed at this time. Add
the vermouth and bring to a boil, stirring constantly. Boil for just a minute or so,
then spoon over the sweetbreads. Serve on anchovy toast. Serves 4.

Anchovy Toast:

½ cup soft butter
2 teaspoons red wine vinegar
2 teaspoons anchovy paste
2 teaspoons chopped parsley
4 slices bread, crusts removed

Mix the butter, wine vinegar, anchovy paste, and parsley. Spread it on both sides
of the bread and bake in a hot oven (425°), turning once so that both sides are
nicely browned—or fry them in a skillet. If there is extra anchovy butter, make a
few fingers of bread in the same manner and serve separately.

Roast Veal in Orange Sauce

This recipe comes from a tennis playing friend—she has more time to spend in the kitchen than we golfers do!

4 pound rump roast of veal
3 tablespoons flour
1 teaspoon salt
2 tablespoons olive oil
1 medium onion, chopped
1 clove garlic, minced
1/3 cup orange juice

grated rind of 1 orange
1/4 teaspoon cinnamon
1/4 cup chopped walnuts
1/2 cup dry sherry
1 cup water
1 teaspoon cornstarch

Rub the flour and salt into the meat. Brown the meat in the oil over high heat until it is crisp all over. Remove it to a heated casserole. Add the onion and garlic to the remaining oil in the pan and sauté until soft. Add the orange juice, orange rind, cinnamon, nuts, and sherry. Bring to a boil. Lower the heat and cook for 1 minute. Pour this sauce over the meat in the casserole. Add the water and simmer over low heat, covered, for 2 hours—or place covered into a 300° oven for 2 hours. Uncover and bake an additional 15 minutes. Remove the meat from the casserole. Skim any fat off the juices and thicken the remaining juice with 1 teaspoon of cornstarch mixed with a bit of water to make a paste. Cook until translucent. Serve this with the meat.

Wiener Schnitzel

1 pound veal cutlets
1 cup very fine bread crumbs
1 egg, beaten
bit of heavy cream
1 clove garlic
1/4 cup butter
1/2 teaspoon salt
1/4 teaspoon pepper
4 thin slices lemon

Pound the cutlets to tenderize them. Dip the veal into the crumbs, then into the beaten egg to which has been added a bit of cream (about 1 tablespoon). Dip into the crumbs again. Rub the frying pan with the garlic. Heat the butter and when hot but not brown, cook the cutlets, browning them carefully on both sides. Cook until tender. Top each cutlet with a slice of lemon. Serve with buttered noodles, a fresh green salad and a stein of German beer! Serves 4.

Poultry and Game

Baked Chicken Salad Sandwiches

A sure hit at any luncheon. To save time, prepare them the day before.

4 chicken breasts, cooked and diced
¼ cup chopped celery
¼ cup chopped green onion
salt and pepper to taste
mayonnaise to moisten
16 ounces cream cheese
4 egg yolks
16 slices bread

Make the chicken salad with the chicken breasts, celery, green onion, salt, pepper, and mayonnaise. Trim the crusts from the bread—use thinly sliced bread. Butter both sides of each slice of bread and fill with the chicken salad. Place on a cookie sheet and frost with the following mixture. Beat the cream cheese with the 4 egg yolks and continue beating until they are fluffy. Frost the tops and sides of the sandwiches with this mixture. Decorate with almonds, although this is not necessary. Cover with foil and refrigerate for 24 hours. Stick some toothpicks into the sandwiches before putting on the foil as the topping will stick to the foil. Remove from the refrigerator 1 hour before baking. Remove the foil and bake in a 325° oven for 30 minutes or until golden. If made ahead, these can be frozen before they are baked. Serves 8.

Chicken Baked in Foil

Perfect for the golfing season. You will want to serve this to your family and friends, for it is inexpensive and you can prepare it ahead of time. Put it into the refrigerator, jump into your golf clothes and forget about the chicken until you get home, then put it into the oven. It waits well in both places. If you have friends who are NEVER on time, this is for them.

1 chicken breast per person
salt and pepper
paprika
oil and butter mixture
green onions
sliced mushrooms
chopped parsley
2 tablespoons heavy cream per serving

Sprinkle the chicken with salt, pepper, and paprika, and sauté in a small amount of an oil and butter mixture until golden. Remove and drain well. Put the chicken on a large piece of aluminum foil. Sauté the green onions, allowing about 1 tablespoon of cooked onions per serving. Place the green onions, a few slices of mushrooms, and a bit of chopped parsley on each breast. Pour 2 tablespoons of heavy cream over each piece of chicken and seal the edges of the foil together tightly. Place into the refrigerator. One hour before serving, place the packages into a shallow baking pan and bake in a 225° oven for 1 hour. Those habitually late friends still not there? Turn the oven down to 200° and the chicken will keep very well.

Chicken and Broccoli Casserole

An old favorite, perfect for a luncheon.

3 to 4 whole chicken breasts
20 ounces broccoli spears
(two 10 ounce packages)
2 cans cream of chicken soup
1 cup Miracle Whip
1 teaspoon lemon juice

½ teaspoon curry powder
½ cup shredded nippy cheese
salt and pepper to taste
½ cup bread crumbs
1 tablespoon melted butter

Cook, bone, and skin the chicken breasts. Cut them in half. This will provide 6 to 8 pieces of chicken. Cook and drain the broccoli. Heat together the soup, Miracle Whip, lemon juice, curry powder, cheese, and salt and pepper to taste. Pour this over alternate layers of chicken and broccoli in a greased casserole dish. Toss the bread crumbs in melted butter and sprinkle them on top of the casserole. Bake ½ hour in a 350° oven. Decorate with strips of pimento—not necessary but attractive. This recipe can be made ahead, and it doubles well. Serves 6.

Chicken Breasts in Cream and Brandy Sauce

Bone and skin the chicken breasts ahead of time, chop the onion, have the lemon juice ready and you can prepare this meal in less than ½ hour. Frozen French-style green beans and some instant rice, a tossed green salad, and here is a meal you could serve with pride—your guests would never know you had been out on the golf course all day.

2 large chicken breasts, skinned, boned and halved
1 tablespoon oil
2 tablespoons butter
salt and pepper to taste
4 green onions, finely chopped
4 tablespoons brandy
½ cup heavy cream
2 egg yolks
1 teaspoon lemon juice

Heat the oil and butter and cook the chicken in it over moderate heat, turning occasionally for 5 minutes. Salt and pepper the breasts first. Add the onions and cook another 5 minutes or until the chicken is done—it doesn't take long when the breasts have been skinned and boned. Transfer to a heated serving platter and keep warm. Add the brandy to the juices in the pan. Bring to a boil and stir to loosen any bits from the bottom of the pan. Reduce the heat and blend in the cream and egg yolks. Simmer very gently until the mixture thickens. Taste, adding lemon juice and additional salt and pepper if necessary. Serves 4.

Chicken Breasts Mandolay

This can be served at a luncheon or dinner. For luncheon, just serve some rice, a tossed green salad or molded salad and hot rolls. For dinner serve the same, only include a vegetable—French-style green beans or peas with sautéed mushrooms.

4 chicken breasts, 8 ounces each
3 tablespoons flour
1 tablespoon curry powder
4 tablespoons vegetable oil
1 teaspoon salt

Bone and halve the chicken breasts. Mix the flour and curry with the chicken in a bag, and shake to coat the chicken. Brown the breasts in the 4 tablespoons of vegetable oil. Place into a large baking dish and cover with the following sauce.

Sauce:

1 medium onion, chopped
1 tablespoon butter
1 cup apricot purée (use strained baby food)
½ teaspoon salt
1 tablespoon curry
4 teaspoons vinegar
2 tablespoons honey

In a saucepan, combine the above ingredients. Bring to a boil. Simmer for 5 minutes then pour over the chicken. Bake covered in a 350° oven for 45 minutes. Serves 4.

Chicken Breasts with Mushroom Sauce

This can be partly made ahead of time.

4 chicken breasts
1 egg
1 tablespoon milk
fine bread crumbs
garlic powder
paprika

butter
box of fresh mushrooms (small size)
1 can consommé
1 can mushroom soup
2 tablespoons sherry
chopped parsley

Skin and bone the chicken breasts. Dry them well. Beat the egg and mix with the milk. Dip the chicken pieces into the egg and milk mixture, then roll in the fine bread crumbs to which have been added a bit of garlic powder and paprika. Brown the chicken in the butter. Put into a casserole—it can be refrigerated at this point if it is being made ahead. Slice the mushrooms and add to the chicken. Mix the consommé, mushroom soup, and sherry, and pour over the chicken. Bake in a 300° oven for 1½ hours. Sprinkle with chopped parsley before serving. Serves 4.

Chicken Breasts with Soufflé Topping

¾ pint thick cream sauce
6 tablespoons grated Swiss Gruyère cheese
2 egg whites, stiffly beaten
8 thin slices cooked ham
4 large chicken breasts, halved, skinned, and boned
salt and pepper to taste

Make the soufflé topping by combining the cream sauce, grated cheese, and stiffly beaten egg whites. In a large shallow baking dish, lay the 8 slices of ham. Sauté the chicken breasts on both sides until cooked—about 10 minutes. Lay the pieces of chicken on the ham slices and top each with the soufflé topping. Bake in a hot oven until the top is puffed and golden brown. Serves 8.

Chicken in Orange

This recipe comes from my cousin in Calgary who is a great cook.

1 broiler, cut up
6 ounce can frozen orange juice
¾ cup water
2 teaspoons grated onion
½ cup melted butter
1 cup corn flake crumbs
2 teaspoons seasoned salt

Wash and dry the chicken. Combine the orange juice, water, and onion in a large bowl and add the chicken, turning to coat it with the marinade. Cover and refrigerate overnight. The next day, dip the chicken pieces into melted butter, then roll in seasoned crumbs. Place on a foil-lined pan. Drizzle the remaining butter over the chicken. It can be put into the refrigerator at this point to be used later. When ready to bake, bake uncovered in a 350° oven for 1 hour or until tender. Garnish with orange slices or kumquats. Serves 4.

Chicken, Spinach, and Cheese Shells

This is one of my favorite recipes. On a recent trip to Toronto I had something similar, loved it, and decided I would try to duplicate it. The particular evening I tried it for the first time, my son had to have dinner early, and one of my daughters decided she was going to start on Weight Watchers. After preparing these two special dinners, I was tired of cooking and I was losing interest in the shells. So rather than making the sauce I had intended, which would have taken me an additional thirty minutes, I simply grated some Mozzarella cheese over the shells, poured a bit of cream over them, sprinkled them with Parmesan cheese, then baked them. The recipe was such a success, I never have tried it with the sauce I had originally planned for this dish.

3 cups pasta shells (large size)
1½ cups finely minced cooked breast of chicken
1 cup finely chopped cooked spinach (12 ounces frozen is roughly 1 cup)
½ cup grated Parmesan cheese
2 eggs, well beaten
¼ cup heavy cream

1 clove garlic, finely minced
½ cup bread crumbs
2 teaspoons minced parsley
¼ teaspoon nutmeg
salt and pepper to taste
1 cup grated Mozzarella cheese
¾ cup heavy cream
¼ to ½ cup grated Parmesan cheese

Boil the shells until tender (about 15 minutes). Stir occasionally but carefully, as the shells must not be broken. Remove from the heat but do not drain. Add enough cold water so that the shells can be handled comfortably. Remove from the water as they are filled. Combine the chicken, spinach, ½ cup Parmesan cheese, eggs, ¼ cup cream, garlic, bread crumbs, parsley, nutmeg, salt, and pepper. Fill the shells with this spinach mixture (about 2 teaspoons filling per shell) and place into a buttered casserole. Don't layer the shells. Sprinkle with the Mozzarella cheese. Pour the cream over (more than the ¾ cup may be desired, depending on the size of the baking dish—just enough is needed to cover the bottom of the dish). Sprinkle with the Parmesan cheese and bake in a 350° oven for 20 to 30 minutes. Makes 75 shells.

Chilean Chicken

This savory dish can be served at small dinner parties or at large buffets. If you are using a smaller amount of chicken, don't cut down on the amount of sauce. I like to have extra sauce to serve hot at the table because it is SO good!

4 to 5 pounds chicken parts
(about 15 pieces)
1 medium onion, finely chopped
1 clove garlic, minced
½ green pepper, finely chopped
¼ cup olive oil
½ cup tomato paste
1 teaspoon salt

1 teaspoon basil
½ teaspoon rosemary
¼ teaspoon oregano
¼ teaspoon Tabasco sauce
2 tablespoons dry mustard
¼ cup Worcestershire sauce
½ cup honey
½ cup dry red wine

Brown the chicken pieces and place into a shallow baking dish, large enough so that the chicken pieces lie side by side—they all should get some of that good sauce! Combine all the other ingredients except for the red wine. Simmer for 20 minutes stirring occasionally. Add the red wine and allow to simmer another 15 minutes. Coat the chicken pieces with this sauce, cover with foil and bake in a 350° oven for 1 hour. Remove the foil and bake another 15 minutes or until done. If making this recipe ahead, brown the chicken pieces, add the sauce, and refrigerate overnight. The next day bake as above.

Curried Chicken

This recipe was given to me years ago by a gal whose husband was in the food services business. It is an excellent recipe and I have made it many times.

1 tablespoon curry powder (Indian)
1 teaspoon ginger
1 teaspoon garlic, minced
¼ teaspoon red pepper, crushed
1 teaspoon tumeric
¼ teaspoon salt
⅛ teaspoon nutmeg
⅛ teaspoon cinnamon

1 teaspoon sugar
milk
2 medium sized onions, chopped
1 tomato, peeled, seeded and chopped
1 can cream of chicken soup
2 pounds cut up chicken, salted
  and peppered

Mix the first 9 ingredients together with a small amount of milk to form a paste. Add the onions and tomato, then the chicken soup, thinning with additional milk until well mixed but not too thin. Pour over the chicken and bake in a 250° oven for about 3 hours. This recipe can be put together in the morning or the night before. Suggested condiments: chopped bananas, chutney, plumped raisins, coconut, peanuts, chopped green onions, and riced hard-boiled eggs (keep whites and yolks separate). Serve the condiments in separate dishes. They can all be assembled ahead of time with the exception of the chopped bananas. Serves 4.

Honeyed Garlic Chicken Wings

Chicken wings are inexpensive and very popular. They are delicious prepared this way.

¼ cup soy sauce
½ cup liquid honey
2 cloves garlic, finely minced
1 teaspoon sherry
2 to 3 pounds chicken wings

Combine the soy sauce, honey, garlic and sherry. Bake the chicken wings in a 350° oven for 1 hour, basting from time to time with the above sauce until all of it is used. Serves 4.

Victor's Chicken

This recipe comes from a bachelor friend of my daughter's. He claims it is the best tasting chicken ever. When he comes home from work, he sticks a potato and this chicken into the oven and 10 minutes before it is finished, he cooks a package of frozen broccoli. He says, "I sit down to dinner and it is so good, I can't believe I made it." He also admits that it is the only thing he knows how to make.

1 package cut up chicken
½ cup ketchup
¼ cup brown sugar
¼ cup water
1 package onion soup mix

Mix together the ketchup, sugar, water, and onion soup mix. Pour this mixture over the chicken pieces. Bake, covered in foil, in a 400° oven for 45 minutes. Remove the foil and bake an additional 15 minutes. Serves 4.

Cornish Game Hens with Tomatoes and Cream

2 Cornish game hens
salt and pepper
2 medium tomatoes, skinned
paprika
½ cup light cream
½ teaspoon oregano

Salt the inside of the birds then stuff them with the tomatoes which have been skinned and quartered. Put the hens into a small pan and sprinkle with paprika, as this gives them a rich brown color when roasted. Bake in a 350° oven for 1 hour or until done. It usually takes just over 1 hour, about 70 minutes. Take the tomatoes out of the birds and add them to the pan. Remove the birds to a heated platter while making the sauce. Remove any excess fat from the pan, and with a fork mash the tomatoes, working them into the pan juices. Add the cream and the oregano and heat to the boiling point. Remove at once and spoon over the hens. Serves 2.

Duck with Orange Sauce

Oranges are the classic flavoring and garnish with duck. I have tried others, all good, but none better than this.

4 to 6 pound duck
salt and pepper
1 orange, sliced
1 cup orange marmalade
½ cup honey

1 teaspoon cinnamon
½ teaspoon cloves
2 teaspoons rosemary
5 tablespoons orange juice

Rub the duck inside and out with salt and pepper. Stuff it with the whole orange cut into slices. Sew up the opening. Prick the fat skin with a fork. Place the duck into a baking dish and bake in a 450° oven for 20 minutes to allow some of the excess fat to escape. Remove the duck from the oven and reduce the temperature to 300°. Pour any fat from the baking dish. Mix the marmalade, honey, cinnamon, cloves and rosemary. Heavily coat the duck with ⅓ of this sauce. Place the baking dish into a pan of hot water (so the sauce won't burn on the bottom)—there should be about 1 inch of water in the outer pan. Bake for an additional 1½ to 2 hours, basting again after the first ½ hour. Remove the duck and let sit for 10 minutes. Add 5 tablespoons of orange juice to the remaining sauce and bring to a boil. Serve the sauce separately. If cooking 2 ducks, double the amount of basting sauce. Serves 4.

Glazed Duck

This is for the woman whose husband hates to carve.

4 to 6 pound duck
salt and pepper to taste
1 jar red currant jelly
1 cup orange juice

Cut the duck into quarters and season it with salt and pepper. Prick the skin so that the fat can run off. Place into a roasting pan and bake for 1 hour in a 350° oven, pouring off the fat at frequent intervals. Meanwhile, melt the currant jelly in the orange juice and bring to a boil. Start basting the duck with this mixture and bake an additional 1 to 1½ hours, basting frequently until all the sauce is used. Serves 3 to 4.

Roast Wild Duck with Apple and Sour Cream Stuffing

3 wild ducks
1½ cups chopped apple
⅓ cup chopped onion
3 tablespoons butter
4 cups soft bread crumbs

2 teaspoons lemon juice
½ teaspoon sage
½ teaspoon salt
3 tablespoons sour cream
  (or enough to moisten)

Apple and Sour Cream Stuffing:

Sauté the apple and onion in butter for 5 minutes. Add to the bread crumbs and mix lightly. Add the lemon juice, sage, and salt. Moisten with the sour cream.

Clean the ducks, removing any pin feathers. Stuff them with the apple and sour cream stuffing, and place on a rack in a roaster. Bake in a 400° oven until brown. This will take 30 to 40 minutes. Then reduce the heat to 250°. Cover the roaster with a lid or foil and bake for 2 hours or until tender. Serve with Red Wine Sauce (see index) or make a gravy from the pan juices. If making gravy, be sure to first pour off all the fat, then add water or stock to the residue in the pan and thicken it with flour mixed with cold water. Salt and pepper to taste. Serves 6.

General John's Roast Pheasant with Brandy Sauce

We were fortunate to live next door to General J. M. Rockingham for several years. Besides being a very famous Canadian soldier, he is an excellent marksman, an expert canoeist, an avid skier, a connoisseur of good food and a not bad golfer! During the hunting season, my husband often accompanied him on 'shoots', becoming a pretty fair shot himself. That is how I gained experience in cooking game birds. General Rockingham's wife is an excellent cook, but when it comes to cooking the General's game, he insists on taking over in the kitchen. Here is his favorite recipe for pheasant. He insists on hanging these birds for at least 10 days because too fresh birds are often tasteless and inclined to be tough.

5 green onions, thinly sliced
2 tablespoons butter
2 pheasants
⅓ cup brandy
1⅓ cups chicken bouillon

freshly ground pepper to taste
4 slices bacon
1⅓ cups heavy cream
1 tablespoon horseradish
⅔ teaspoon salt

Sauté the green onions in butter in a roasting pan for 5 minutes. Add the pheasants and sauté over high heat until brown on all sides. Pour some brandy into a ladle, then pour the rest over the pheasants. Warm the ladle slightly, light it and flame the pheasants. When the flames die, add the bouillon, salt, and pepper. Place the bacon on the pheasants' breasts and roast uncovered in a 375° oven for 45 minutes, basting frequently. Stir the cream and horseradish into the pan juices and continue roasting for 15 minutes, basting frequently. Serves 6.

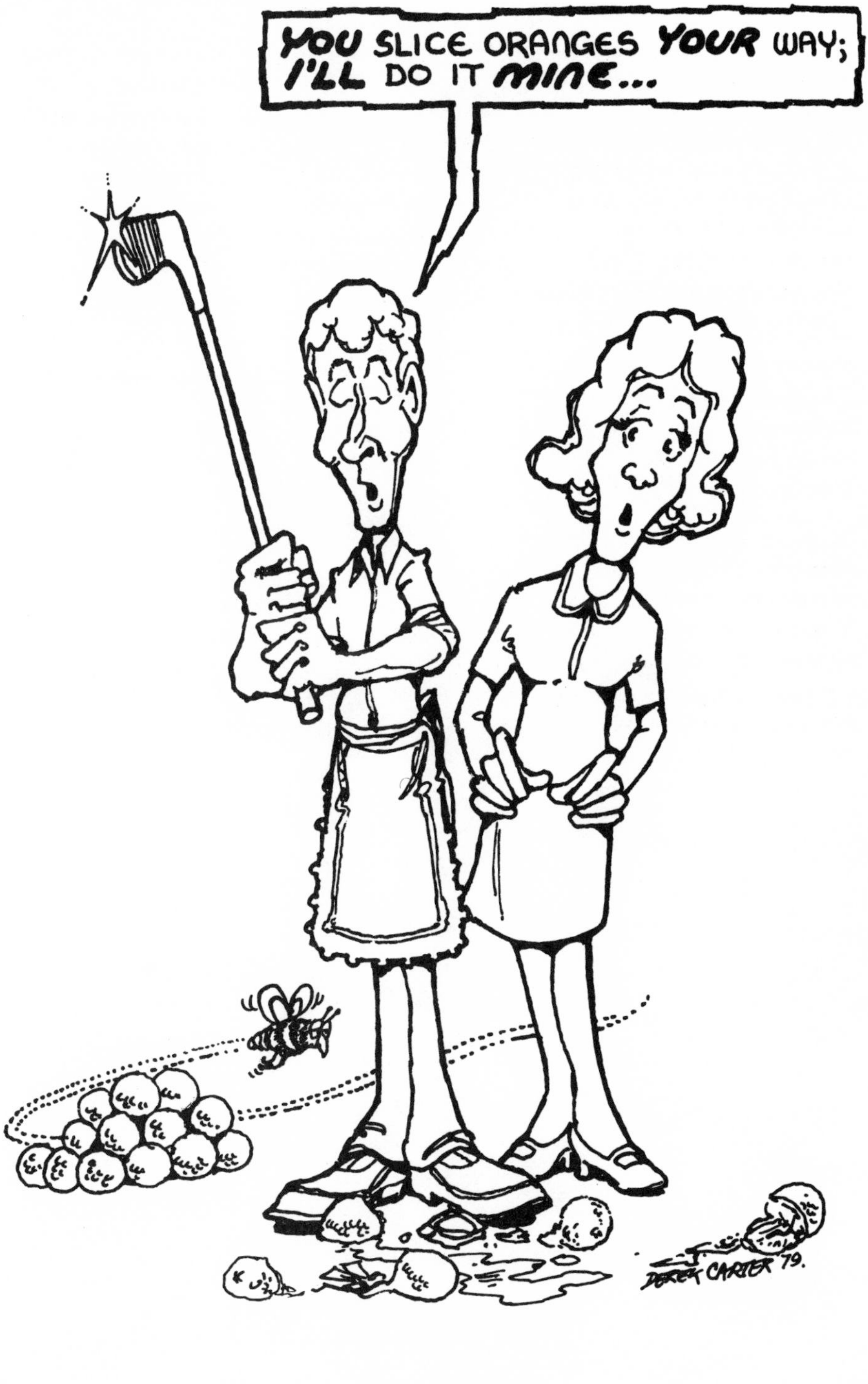
YOU SLICE ORANGES YOUR WAY; I'LL DO IT MINE...
DEREK CARTER '79.

Eggs and Cheese

Artichoke Omelet

*Our neighbors, the Mortimer-Lambs, give the most magnificent breakfast
parties. They always serve something interesting and it is served beautifully.
The last time we were there, they served the following artichoke omelet. It was
preceded by champagne with orange juice and wedges of fresh assorted melons.
It was followed by freshly baked croissants and wild strawberry preserves.*

3 tablespoons butter
1 cup artichoke hearts, drained and coarsely chopped
   (or use frozen artichoke hearts)
½ cup fresh mushrooms, chopped
dash of pepper
4 eggs, separated
2 tablespoons water
¼ teaspoon salt

Melt 2 tablespoons of the butter in a small saucepan. Add the artichokes,
mushrooms, and pepper. Cook and stir until hot. Remove from the heat and
keep warm. Beat the egg whites until frothy. Add the water and salt to the egg
whites gradually. Beat until stiff but not dry. Beat the yolks until they are very
thick and lemon colored. Fold them into the egg whites. Heat the remaining 1
tablespoon of butter in a 10 inch oven-proof skillet. Pour the egg mixture into
the skillet and spread it evenly, leaving it a little higher at the sides. Bake in a
325° oven for 10 minutes. Reduce the heat to 300° and bake for an additional 5
to 8 minutes, until the omelet is puffed and set, or until a knife inserted into the
center comes out clean. Loosen the sides of the omelet with a spatula. Place the
artichoke mixture on half of the omelet. Fold the omelet over and turn out onto
a warm platter. Serve with Blender Hollandaise Sauce (see index). Serves 4.

Cheese Omelet

½ package Velveeta cheese (8 ounce size)
¼ cup cream
6 tablespoons butter
6 eggs, separated
pinch of salt

Melt the cheese in the top of a double boiler. Add the cream and blend well. Melt the butter in a large 10 inch frying pan (cast iron is the best). Beat the egg yolks, adding salt. Blend the cheese mixture with the yolks, beating well. Beat the egg whites until they are stiff and fold them into the cheese mixture. Pour into the hot buttered pan and cook over a low heat until the omelet is set on the bottom. Place into a 350° oven and bake 10 to 15 minutes or until cooked. Serves 4.

Overnight Cheese Soufflé

The last time I made this, I covered it with plastic wrap before putting it into the refrigerator. The next day, I rushed in from a golf game and stuck it into the oven, my mind reflecting on the one good drive I had had during my 18 hole otherwise disaster. I ran up for a quick shower before cooking the sausages and preparing the salad. When I brought the casserole to the table, the children all asked, "How did you get it so shiny, Mom?" That's right, I forgot to take off the plastic wrap.

10 slices white bread
½ pound Cheddar cheese, grated
4 eggs
2⅔ cups milk
salt, pepper, and paprika

Trim the crusts from the bread. Butter a casserole (oblong is best), and put half the bread on the bottom. Sprinkle with half the cheese, then lay a second layer of bread. Spread this second layer with the rest of the cheese. Beat the eggs. Add the milk, salt, pepper, and paprika. Pour over the bread and cheese in the casserole. Set the casserole into a pan of hot water and bake in a 350° oven for 1 hour, or until set. Serve immediately. Serves 4 to 6, depending on what is being served with the soufflé.

David's Eggs

Do you have a foursome for next Sunday's golf game? Invite them for breakfast before you head for the links, and serve these eggs. Some brown or whole wheat toast, some hot coffee, and off you go. Remember—no slicing or hooking!

4 thin slices ham	4 eggs
4 thin slices Swiss cheese	½ cup heavy cream
1 green pepper, seeded and diced	4 tablespoons butter, melted
2 tomatoes, peeled, seeded and diced	salt and pepper to taste
2 tablespoons butter	Parmesan cheese to sprinkle on top

Line four buttered au gratin dishes, or individual casseroles, with 1 slice of ham and 1 slice of Swiss cheese. Sauté the green pepper and tomatoes in butter until they are soft. Spoon out these vegetables equally around the sides of the 4 dishes and break 1 egg into the middle of each dish. Cover with 2 or 3 tablespoons of the cream and 1 tablespoon of the melted butter. Season with salt and pepper. Sprinkle the Parmesan cheese on top. Preheat the oven to 350° and put the dishes on the middle rack. Immediately turn the oven down to 250° and bake 15 to 20 minutes. Serves 4.

Eggs Suisse

These are cooked in the same manner as David's Eggs (see index). They are a little more simple to prepare and are definitely classified 'special.'

butter
package of Swiss cheese (individually foil wrapped wedges)
2 eggs per person
Parmesan cheese (about ¼ cup per serving)
1 or 2 teaspoons heavy cream per egg

Preheat oven to 350°. In each of individual baking dishes, spread a thin layer of butter. Cut the Swiss cheese into bits and spread some in the bottom of each dish. Crack 2 eggs on top of the cheese and sprinkle the Parmesan cheese over the eggs. Put a teaspoon (should be enough) of heavy cream on each egg. Lower oven temperature to 250° and bake for 15 to 20 minutes or until the yolks are set. Serves 1.

Margaret's Cheese Pie

My neighbor Margaret Otto serves this delicious cheese pie. It is perfect for a brunch or luncheon. You can make the filling the day before and store it in the refrigerator. The next day, just fill the pie shell and bake. For a luncheon or light supper, just serve with bacon and/or sausage and a tossed salad. For brunch, omit the salad. You could also serve it at a dinner party with baked ham or a bland fish such as sole or halibut.

9 inch pie shell
1 pound sharp Cheddar cheese, grated
1 cup unflavored yogurt
¼ teaspoon nutmeg
2 tablespoons finely chopped onion

1 teaspoon sugar
4 eggs, well beaten
salt and pepper to taste
¼ cup Parmesan cheese

Partially bake the pie shell—prick the bottom first and bake in a 400° oven for 5 to 8 minutes. Gently push the bottom down with the back of a fork if it bubbles up. Mix together the grated cheese, yogurt, nutmeg, onion, and sugar. Add the well beaten eggs, salt, and pepper. Beat again until the ingredients are well blended. Pour into the pie shell and sprinkle the top with the grated Parmesan cheese. Bake in a 350° oven for 45 minutes or until the top is brown and puffy. Serves 6.

Quiche Lorraine

10 inch partially baked pie shell
1 cup crisp bacon bits
1 cup Gruyère or Swiss cheese, cubed
4 eggs plus 1 yolk, beaten lightly together
1½ cups light cream
½ teaspoon salt
dash of pepper
dash of cayenne
⅛ teaspoon nutmeg
1 can French fried onion rings (optional)

Sprinkle the bottom of the partially baked pie shell with the bacon and cubed cheese. Mix together the eggs, cream, salt, pepper, cayenne, and nutmeg. Pour this mixture over the bacon and cheese. Sprinkle the top with (canned) French fried onion rings at this time, if desired. Bake in a 375° oven for 30 to 35 minutes or until a knife inserted into the middle comes out clean. Serves 6.

Scrambled Eggs with Smoked Salmon

Try this for a real gourmet breakfast!

6 eggs
⅛ teaspoon salt
pinch of white pepper
¼ pound smoked salmon
¼ cup milk
1 tablespoon butter
chopped parsley

Beat the eggs slightly and add the salt and pepper. Cut the salmon into small pieces and add to the eggs with the ¼ cup milk. Melt the butter in a skillet and add the egg mixture. Stir slowly over medium heat until cooked. Garnish with chopped parsley. Serves 3 to 4.

Vegetables

Baked Bananas

I often wonder why more people don't serve bananas as a vegetable. They are so good for you—full of potassium—so my mother says, who eats a small one every day and at 70 years of age looks marvellous. Be sure to buy slightly under-ripe bananas when using them as a vegetable.

4 bananas
1 beaten egg
1½ teaspoons salt
½ cup cornflake crumbs
3 tablespoons butter or margarine, melted

Peel the bananas and cut in half crosswise. Dip them into the egg, to which the salt has been added. Drain on a rack for 2 to 3 minutes. Roll in the crumbs until coated. Place on a greased cookie sheet and sprinkle with the melted butter. Bake in a 400° oven for about 10 minutes or until golden brown and the bananas are tender. Serve with ham, pork, or spicy chicken dishes.

Overnight Barley and Mushroom Casserole

Good with beef, ham, or pork.

5 tablespoons butter
2 onions, chopped
½ pound mushrooms, thinly sliced
3 slices bacon, crumbled

1½ cups pot barley
5 cups consommé
¼ teaspoon thyme
salt and pepper to taste

Melt 3 tablespoons of the butter in a skillet and sauté the onions for 5 minutes. Add the mushrooms and sauté an additional 3 minutes. Transfer to a casserole and add the crumbled bacon. Add the remaining 2 tablespoons of butter to the skillet and brown the barley. Add to the mushrooms, bacon, and onions in the casserole. Add the seasonings and consommé. Stir to mix. Cover and bake in a 350° oven for 1 hour. Let sit in the refrigerator overnight. Bake an additional 30 minutes in a 350° oven before serving. Serves 8.

Harvard Beets

Nice with ham, pork, or chicken.

14 ounces whole baby beets (canned) 2 teaspoons vinegar
2 tablespoons butter   ¼ teaspoon salt
2 tablespoons flour   dash of pepper
¼ teaspoon onion juice   1½ teaspoons sugar

Drain the beets, saving the liquid. Melt the butter and blend in the flour. Slowly add the beet juice and stir constantly over direct heat until the sauce boils and thickens. Add the remaining ingredients and the beets and continue heating slowly until the beets are hot throughout. Serve at once. Serves 4.

Broccoli Casserole

This is much like the recipe for Mary's Broccoli Casserole (see index). It is not easy to cut that particular recipe in half, so if I am entertaining a smaller group but still need a green 'make ahead' vegetable dish that will serve 10 to 12, I use this recipe.

1 to 2 pound package frozen chopped broccoli
1 box Uncle Ben's Rice and Wild Rice Mixture
2 tins cream of mushroom soup
1 pound jar Cheez Whiz
1 can water chestnuts, sliced
grated Cheddar cheese

Cook the broccoli and drain. Prepare the rice as directed on the package. Mix everything together except the cheese. Sprinkle the top with enough grated cheese to cover it. Bake in a 350° oven for 1 hour. This recipe can be prepared ahead of time. Serves 10 to 12.

Broccoli with Cream Sauce

16 ounces frozen broccoli spears
2 tablespoons butter
2 tablespoons flour
1 cup milk
½ cup sour cream
¼ teaspoon salt, or to taste
½ cup buttered bread crumbs
½ cup Parmesan cheese

Cook the broccoli. Drain and put into a buttered 6 by 9 inch pan. Make the sauce with the flour, butter, and milk. Fold in the sour cream and add salt to taste, about ¼ teaspoon. Pour over the broccoli in the pan and sprinkle with a mixture of bread crumbs and Parmesan cheese. Bake in a 350° oven for about 20 to 25 minutes or until the crumbs are nicely browned. Serves 6.

Mary's Broccoli Casserole

This comes from my friend Mary Fullerton who often has to entertain large crowds. That fact plus six children is why she doesn't have time to play golf any more. The last time I played golf with Mary, she was eight months pregnant. She was hitting the ball beautifully—but she had to get someone else to tee it up!

4 pounds frozen chopped broccoli
1 package long grain and wild rice mix, 6 ounce size
1 cup Minute Rice
1 pound jar Cheez Whiz
3 cans cream of mushroom soup
garlic bread crumbs

Cook the broccoli as directed. Cook the rice as directed. Beat the soup and cheese together. Mix all together and put into a large greased casserole. Sprinkle the top with buttered crumbs and bake in a 350° oven for 1 hour. Can be made the night before. Serves 20. To serve 10, see Broccoli Casserole recipe, in index.

Savoy Cabbage

For years I passed up this wonderful vegetable, simply because I didn't know how to prepare it.

1 head savoy cabbage
2 tablespoons butter
1 small onion, minced
1½ tablespoons flour
liquid from cooked cabbage to make 1 cup
pinch of nutmeg
salt and pepper to taste

Boil the whole head of cabbage until soft (approximately 15-20 minutes). Drain and save the liquid. Sauté the onion in butter and when soft, add the flour. Stir in 1 cup of the cabbage liquid (if not enough, add water to make 1 cup). Cook and stir the mixture until it thickens. Add a pinch of nutmeg and salt and pepper to taste. Chop the cabbage and combine it with the sauce. Put into a casserole and keep warm in the oven.

Carrot Asparagus Casserole

One of my mother's good friends in Vancouver is an excellent cook. When Mother visits me, Marge always sends with her one of her recipes because she knows I love to cook and that I enjoy good food.

16 ounces frozen asparagus (use fresh if in season)
2 pound package frozen carrot slices
1 onion, minced
2 boxes fresh mushrooms
2 tablespoons melted butter

Cook the asparagus and carrots separately. Sauté the onion and mushrooms in melted butter until they start to brown. Put the carrots into a large buttered casserole. Arrange the asparagus on top of the carrots. Cover the carrots and asparagus with the sautéed mushrooms and onions. Cover with the following sauce:

4 tablespoons butter
4 tablespoons flour
2 cups milk
1 teaspoon Worcestershire sauce
½ pound sharp Cheddar cheese, grated
salt and pepper

Melt the butter. Add the flour. Gradually add the milk, stirring constantly. When thickened, remove from the heat and stir in the grated cheese. Salt and pepper to taste. Pour this sauce over the vegetables in the casserole and bake for 30 minutes in a 350° oven. This recipe can be cut in half. Serves 18 to 20.

Carrots Grand Marnier

This is a very simple recipe. It comes in handy when you are planning a special dinner and looking for a vegetable other than a green one. When planning a menu, color is very important. Meals must have eye appeal as well as taste appeal, because visual experiences satisfy our senses as much as savory experiences. You can vary the amounts of this dish according to the number you are serving. Make it for 6 or 60—although I have never made it for as many as 60!

1½ pounds carrots
2 to 3 tablespoons butter
salt and pepper to taste
pinch of nutmeg
2 to 3 tablespoons Grand Marnier liqueur (according to taste)

Cook the carrots. Mash them with butter (vary the amount of butter according to taste, but it should be fairly buttery). Add salt, pepper, and nutmeg to taste. Stir in the Grand Marnier. To make this recipe ahead, mix everything but the Grand Marnier. Reheat, then add the Grand Marnier just before serving. Serves 6.

Puffy Parmesan Cauliflower

This recipe is so attractive, tasty, and flexible. Having more guests? Add another head of cauliflower and increase the amount of sauce!

1 medium cauliflower
milk and water, equally mixed, for cooking
½ cup mayonnaise
¼ cup grated Parmesan cheese
2 tablespoons chopped parsley
1 tablespoon fresh lemon juice
¼ teaspoon salt
2 egg whites, stiffly beaten

Trim the cauliflower and cook it in a mixture of half milk and half water until tender. Milk helps keep the cauliflower white. Watch that it doesn't boil over—use a deep pot. Drain the cauliflower and place it stem down into a shallow baking dish. Combine the mayonnaise, grated cheese, parsley, lemon juice, and salt. Beat the egg whites until they are stiff and fold into the mayonnaise mixture. Spread over the cooked cauliflower. Broil 6 to 8 inches from the heat until the sauce is puffed and golden brown. Rotate it half way through to keep it evenly browned. Serves 6.

Eggplant Casserole

This is a bit time consuming, but believe me it is worth it. Put it together the night before then bake it for 1 hour before you serve it.

½ cup cooking oil, maybe a little more
2 onions, chopped
2 large green peppers, chopped
1 clove garlic, minced
2 eggplants, cut into ½ inch slices
salt and pepper to taste

2 cups grated Cheddar cheese
1 can mushroom soup
1 can tomato sauce (14 ounces)
½ teaspoon chili powder
1 teaspoon Worcestershire sauce
buttered bread crumbs

Sauté the onions, green peppers, and garlic until tender. Remove them from the pan then fry the eggplant slices lightly—drain on absorbent paper. Butter a large baking dish and cover with a layer of the eggplant. Sprinkle the eggplant with some of the onions and green peppers, salt, pepper, and grated cheese. Repeat the layers until all is used up. Mix together the mushroom soup, tomato sauce, chili powder, and Worcestershire sauce and spread over top of the casserole. Refrigerate at this point if making recipe ahead of time. Just before baking, cover with buttered bread crumbs, dot with butter, and bake in a 375° oven for 1 hour. Serves 12 to 14.

Baked Eggplant Slices

1 large eggplant, or 2 small
salted water
1 cup instant mashed potato flakes
½ cup grated Parmesan cheese
2 eggs, lightly beaten
melted butter, to cover bottom of cookie sheet

Cut ¼ inch slices of the eggplant and soak in salted water (2 cups water mixed with 2 tablespoons salt) for 1 hour. Drain and dry. Mix the potato flakes and Parmesan cheese in a plastic bag. Dip the eggplant slices into the egg and shake in the potato flake/cheese mixture to coat them well. Place on a well buttered cookie sheet and bake 15 minutes in a 350° oven. Turn and bake another 15 minutes or until golden brown.

Baked Mushrooms

Men love these!

1 clove garlic, minced
1 onion, grated
2 tablespoons parsley, chopped
⅛ teaspoon basil
1 teaspoon salt
¼ teaspoon pepper

⅓ cup olive oil
2 tablespoons wine vinegar
1½ pounds fresh mushrooms, sliced
¼ pound butter
½ cup bread crumbs
1 tablespoon grated Parmesan cheese

Combine the garlic, onion, parsley, basil, salt, pepper, oil, and vinegar in a bowl. Add the mushrooms and allow them to marinate 3 hours, basting frequently. Drain. Melt half the butter in a skillet. Add the mushrooms and cook for 10 minutes, stirring frequently. Butter a baking dish very well and place the mushrooms in it. Sprinkle the bread crumbs and cheese on top and dot with the remaining butter. Place under the broiler until brown.

Scalloped Onions

6 medium onions, peeled and sliced thinly
¼ cup butter
¼ cup flour
1½ cups milk
1 teaspoon Worcestershire sauce
½ teaspoon salt
1 teaspoon paprika
2 cups grated sharp Cheddar cheese

Separate the onions into rings and place them into a well buttered shallow baking dish. Melt the butter and blend in the flour. Gradually add the milk and cook until liquid thickens. Stir in the Worcestershire sauce, salt, paprika, and cheese. Stir until the cheese has melted. Pour this mixture over the onions and bake in a 350° oven for 1 hour. Serves 8.

Deep Fried Parsley

I use this to garnish fish dishes. It is particularly nice with sole which can be very boring if care is not given to its preparation.

1 or 2 bunches parsley
fat or oil for deep frying

Wash the parsley. Shake and dry it extremely well on paper towels. Make sure no water remains on the parsley, or the fat in which you fry it will spatter. Heat the frying fat or oil to 375°. Put the parsley into a frying basket and drop it into the hot fat. Fry only until the parsley surfaces and has become crisp. This will take only 10 to 15 seconds. Do not over fry or the color will change. Drain on paper towels and serve immediately.

Glazed Parsnips

My favorite way of cooking parsnips is to just throw them into the pan with the roast. When I do this, I throw in two. The first one is for me and the second one is for me. I can't find anyone in the family who shares my enthusiasm. However, since they all like sweet things, I find they will eat parsnips if I prepare them in the following manner.

8 parsnips
6 tablespoons butter
⅓ cup brown sugar, firmly packed
⅔ cup apple cider
1 teaspoon salt

Peel the parsnips, cut them into quarters lengthwise and trim out any woody core. Cook them in boiling salted water until tender when tested with a fork. Drain thoroughly. Lay the parsnips in a shallow baking dish. Mix together the butter, brown sugar, cider, and salt. Spoon this mixture over the parsnips and bake in a 400° oven for 20 to 25 minutes, basting occasionally until they are nicely glazed. Serves 6 to 8.

Pea Timbales with Carrot Cream Sauce

1 cup pea pulp (sieved peas)
2 eggs
few drops onion juice
dash of white pepper
2 tablespoons milk

1 tablespoon melted butter
½ teaspoon salt
2 cups medium cream sauce
½ cup cooked carrots, finely diced

Combine all the ingredients except the cream sauce and carrots. Fill buttered timbale molds (or small muffin tins) with this mixture, set them in a pan of water and bake in a 350° oven until firm. Add the carrots to the cream sauce. Unmold the timbales and cover them with the carrot cream sauce.

Easy Potato Bake

This is a favorite of mine during the golfing season—no peeling, no chopping (or slicing) of potatoes. You can double or triple this recipe very easily. Perfect for a large crowd and SO tasty. You can mix this in the morning and refrigerate it until ready to bake.

1 pound package frozen hash brown potatoes
1¼ cups grated sharp Cheddar cheese (save the ¼ cup for topping)
1 cup sour cream
4 green onions, chopped, tops included
½ cup milk
¾ teaspoon salt
¼ teaspoon pepper

Combine all the ingredients except ¼ cup of the grated cheese. Put into a lightly buttered casserole. (It is not necessary to thaw the potatoes first unless making a large quantity—then let the potatoes thaw slightly for easier mixing.) Top with the reserved cheese. Bake in a 325° oven for 45 minutes to 1 hour. Serves 4 to 6.

Note: if you double this – add 1 tin cream of mushroom soup.

Make Ahead Mashed Potatoes

3 cups mashed potatoes
2 eggs, well beaten
½ cup cream
salt and pepper to taste
3½ ounces (1 can) French fried onion rings (optional)

Add the eggs, cream, and salt and pepper to the mashed potatoes and beat until light and fluffy. Turn into a buttered casserole. Refrigerate, but remove at least one hour before baking. Just before baking, sprinkle the top with onion rings. Bake in a 350° oven for about 30 minutes. Serves 6.

Potatoes Milano

This is an excellent potato dish if you are having a large crowd. You can make this early in the day, then let it sit in the refrigerator until you are ready to bake it. Doubled, it will serve 20 people.

1 large onion, sliced
2 tablespoons butter
⅓ cup butter
⅓ cup flour
4 cups milk
¼ teaspoon garlic powder
1½ teaspoons salt
¼ teaspoon pepper
¾ cup grated Parmesan cheese
2 pound package frozen French fries

Sauté the onion in 2 tablespoons of butter until soft. Set aside. Melt the ⅓ cup of butter. Add the flour and gradually stir in the milk, garlic powder, salt, and pepper. Cook until it starts to thicken. Add the Parmesan cheese and stir until smooth. (Use a wire whisk if necessary.) Add the sautéed onion. Gently mix together the sauce and French fries. Put into a baking dish and bake for 1 hour at 325°. Serves 8 to 10.

Sheila's Potato Pie

Sheila's husband John plays golf but Sheila doesn't, which is why she has time to stay home and make good things like this.

16 ounces cottage cheese
2 cups unseasoned mashed potatoes (no milk added)
½ cup sour cream
2 eggs
1¾ teaspoons salt
⅛ teaspoon cayenne
½ cup green onions, thinly sliced
10 inch pie crust, unbaked
3 tablespoons grated Parmesan cheese

Put everything into a blender except the onions and Parmesan cheese. Blend, then mix in the onions. The filling can be made the morning or the night before, but don't fill the pie shell until it is ready to bake. Pour the filling into the pie shell. Sprinkle with the Parmesan cheese. Bake for 20 minutes in a 425° oven, then an additional 45 minutes or until set, at 375°.

Potatoes Romanoff

8 ounces sour cream
1 cup cream style cottage cheese
½ cup shredded sharp Cheddar cheese
1 teaspoon salt
2 teaspoons horseradish
2 tablespoons chopped parsley
½ cup chopped green onion
6 cups cubed cooked potatoes

Combine the sour cream, cottage cheese, half the shredded cheese, salt, horseradish, parsley, and green onion. Add the potato cubes and toss gently to coat them. Turn into a greased shallow baking dish. (Mixture can be refrigerated at this point.) Bake uncovered in a 325° oven for 30 to 40 minutes. Top with the remaining shredded cheese and return to the oven until the cheese melts, about an additional 5 minutes. Serves 8.

Sweet Potato and Apple Casserole

This delicious mixture of sweet potatoes and tart apples is perfect with roast goose or roast pork.

2 pounds sweet potatoes (5 or 6)
1½ pounds cooking apples
⅔ cup light brown sugar
4 to 6 tablespoons butter
½ cup apple cider

3 tablespoons maple syrup
1 tablespoon lemon juice
1 teaspoon cinnamon
½ teaspoon ginger
1½ to 2 teaspoons cornstarch

Cook the potatoes in their skins in enough water to cover them. When they have cooled, peel and cut them into ¼ inch thick pieces. Peel the apples, cut them into quarters and slice ¼ inch thick. Set them in water which has a bit of lemon juice added, to avoid discoloration. In a small saucepan bring the sugar, butter, cider, syrup, lemon juice, cinnamon, ginger, and cornstarch to a boil. Lower the heat and simmer for 10 minutes. Drain the apples and pat them dry. Arrange overlapping slices of apple and sweet potato in a buttered 2 quart baking dish. Pour sauce over them all. Bake in a 325° oven for 25 to 30 minutes or until the apples are tender. Baste occasionally. Serves 12.

Steamed Radishes

These are really fun to serve because nobody ever knows what they are—they lose their color when they are cooked.

3 bunches radishes
¼ cup butter
1 cup chopped green onions
salt and pepper to taste

Wash and trim the radishes, leaving a bit of the stem untrimmed. Melt the butter in a skillet and sauté the green onions until they are soft. Add the radishes and about ⅓ cup of water. Cover the pan and bring to a high steam. Lower the heat at once and continue steaming the radishes for about 5 minutes or until they are tender. Drain. Season with salt and pepper to taste and add a little additional butter if desired.

Baked Rice

Super easy and great tasting. Perfect for a buffet or to accompany chicken or ham.

1 can whole mushrooms (drained, but keep juice)
1 cup rice, uncooked
½ package Lipton onion soup
2 tablespoons soy sauce
⅛ cup oil
chopped parsley

Measure the liquid from the mushrooms and add water to make 2 cups. Put into a covered casserole and mix in the remaining ingredients. Bake for 1 hour in a 350° oven. The mushrooms will probably float to the top—it's okay, they are supposed to. Sprinkle chopped parsley on top. Serves 6. Triple to serve 16 to 18.

Chinese Fried Rice

A French-Canadian girl gave me this recipe twenty-three years ago. I think I made it every night for two weeks until my husband cried, "Enough!" French-Canadians are not noted for their Chinese cooking, but I sure love this rice.

3 tablespoons salad oil
1 egg
½ onion or 2 green onions, chopped
3 stalks celery, chopped
½ green pepper, chopped
2 tablespoons soy sauce
1 tablespoon Worcestershire sauce
½ teaspoon oregano
freshly ground pepper to taste
3 cups cooked rice
½ tomato, chopped

In a skillet fry 1 egg, lightly beaten, in 3 tablespoons of oil. Lift the edges and let any uncooked egg run underneath until it is set. Remove the egg, cut it into thin strips and set aside. To the oil remaining in the skillet add the onion, celery, green pepper, soy sauce, Worcestershire sauce, oregano, and pepper. Cook 3 to 4 minutes. Add the rice, chopped tomato, and cooked egg shreds, and combine the mixture well. Serves 4.

Lynn's Parmesan Spaghetti

This is the way my daughter prepares spaghetti and it is delicious. If she is really hungry, she puts meat sauce on it, but believe me it doesn't need it.

1 pound spaghetti, cooked and drained
½ pound bacon, lean
2 cloves garlic, minced
3 eggs
1 cup Parmesan cheese
½ cup chopped parsley
salt and pepper to taste

While the spaghetti is cooking, prepare the rest of the ingredients. Dice the bacon and fry slowly until it is golden brown. Add the garlic. Meanwhile, beat the eggs and add the cheese. When the spaghetti is cooked, drain and add the cheese and egg mixture. Toss quickly and gently until all the spaghetti strands are coated. The heat from the spaghetti cooks the egg yolks and melts the cheese so it sticks to the spaghetti. Add the bacon, garlic, and parsley. Check the seasoning. It will probably need only pepper as the spaghetti should have been cooked in salted water. Serve at once, with extra Parmesan served separately. Serves 6.

Spinach Crêpes

These crêpes keep very well in the fridge as I have made them up to four days before using them. I hide a Teflon frying pan from the rest of the family so it won't get scratched and I use it only for crêpes. If you have a crêpe pan, so much the better.

1 cup flour
½ cup water
½ cup milk
2 eggs
2 tablespoons melted butter
¼ teaspoon salt
1 cup cooked spinach

Into the container of a blender put the flour, water, milk, eggs, melted butter, and salt. Add the spinach and blend the batter until smooth. Lightly oil a hot skillet or crêpe pan. Pour in 1 generous tablespoon of the batter then quickly tilt and rotate the pan so that the batter spreads out in a thin layer. Cook for about 30 seconds, turn it over carefully and cook the other side until set, about another 30 seconds. Continue in this manner until all the batter is used up. Stack the crêpes, wrap them well, and store in the refrigerator until ready to use.

With Ham and Cheese Filling:

If I am serving crêpes as a luncheon dish I serve them in the following manner—although I have used them for a buffet in conjunction with another meat dish, such as beef or chicken.

Lay a thin slice of baked ham on each crêpe and top the ham with a small piece of Swiss cheese. Roll up the crêpe and place it in a shallow, flat, oven-proof dish. Sprinkle the crêpes with a bit of melted butter and grated Parmesan cheese. Bake in a 400° oven until the cheese has started to melt and the tops are lightly glazed.

With Chopped Mushroom Filling:

In a saucepan, cook 2 green onions, finely chopped, in 2 tablespoons of butter for 1 or 2 minutes. Add ½ pound of mushrooms, finely chopped, and cook them over low heat, stirring frequently for about 10 minutes. Stir in 1 cup of fresh bread crumbs, 1 teaspoon chopped parsley, and salt and pepper to taste. Fill the crêpes and bake only until they are heated throughout. Cover with Mornay sauce.

Spinach Royale

20 ounces frozen chopped spinach
8 ounces sour cream
1 package onion soup mix
1 egg, beaten
bread crumbs
¼ cup grated Swiss cheese

Mix together the spinach, sour cream, soup mix, and egg. Mix them well and put into a buttered casserole. Sprinkle the top with the bread crumbs mixed with grated cheese. Bake in a 350° oven for about 20 minutes. Serves 6.

Baked Acorn Squash Rings

1 large acorn squash
2 tablespoons melted butter
salt
¼ cup corn syrup

Early in the day wash the acorn squash and cut it into 1 inch thick rings. Brush them with the melted butter and sprinkle with salt. Lay them flat on a cookie sheet and refrigerate. About 40 minutes before serving, bake the squash rings in a 400° oven for 20 minutes. Turn and brush with ¼ cup white corn syrup and bake another 20 minutes or until tender. Fill the centers with peas. Serves 4.

Baked Cherry Tomatoes

Don't try to make these for a large party—it is too tiresome peeling that many tomatoes. If you are just having two to four guests, try these, they are very good. Don't over cook the tomatoes, as you want them to retain their shape. Be sure to pour boiling water over them for a few seconds so the skins will come off easily.

package of cherry tomatoes
½ lemon
several dashes Tabasco sauce
salt and pepper
½ onion, chopped
chopped parsley or chopped chives

Peel the cherry tomatoes and place them into a baking dish. Mix together the lemon juice, Tabasco, salt, and pepper. Pour it over the tomatoes. Sprinkle the chopped onion and chives or parsley on top of the tomatoes. Bake, covered, in a 350° oven until just heated through (10 to 15 minutes). Serves 4.

Baked Tomatoes

I have made both the following recipes for the same party, alternating the brown and the white on the serving dish. It makes a very colorful and attractive combination.

Baked Tomatoes with Cornflake Topping:

4 firm tomatoes
garlic salt
¼ cup butter
¾ cup cornflake crumbs

Cut the tomatoes in half, sprinkle them with garlic salt and place into a buttered baking dish. Melt the butter and mix with the cornflake crumbs. Spread on top of the tomatoes and pack down lightly. Bake in a 350° oven for 20 minutes. Don't over cook or the tomatoes will lose their shape and be difficult to handle.

Baked Tomatoes with Green Pepper and Green Onion Topping:

4 firm tomatoes
celery salt
¾ cup mayonnaise
2 tablespoons chopped green onion
2 tablespoons chopped green pepper

Cut the tomatoes in half, sprinkle them with celery salt and place into a buttered glass pie plate. Top with a mixture of the mayonnaise, green onion, and green pepper. Bake in a 325° oven for 20 minutes. Half a tomato is usually sufficient per person so both of these recipes will serve 8.

Tomatoes with Chopped Mushroom Filling

Perfect with broiled chops.

6 medium firm tomatoes
2 tablespoons butter
3 cups chopped mushrooms
½ cup dry bread crumbs
2 well beaten eggs
1 tablespoon chopped parsley

2 tablespoons chopped chives
½ teaspoon salt
¼ teaspoon black pepper
1 teaspoon curry powder, scant
pinch of dry mustard

Wash the tomatoes and carefully scoop out their insides, leaving hollow shells. Put upside-down on a double thickness of paper towels to drain. Meanwhile, melt the butter and sauté the chopped mushrooms until tender. Add the bread crumbs and cool slightly. Add the well beaten eggs, the parsley, chives, salt, pepper, curry powder, and dry mustard. Mix well and fill the tomato shells with this mixture. Place into a buttered glass pie plate and bake in a 375° oven for 15 to 20 minutes. Serves 6.

Herb Scalloped Tomatoes

3 tablespoons butter
4 slices whole wheat bread, toasted
   and cut into cubes
2 cans stewed tomatoes
   (14 ounce size)
1 teaspoon parsley flakes
½ teaspoon basil

1½ teaspoons instant minced onion
1 teaspoon sugar
½ teaspoon salt
2 ounces blue cheese
Parmesan cheese

Melt the butter and add the toast cubes. Toss well. (When in a hurry, just butter the toast before cutting into cubes.) Mix together the tomatoes, parsley flakes, basil, onion, sugar, and salt. Arrange alternate layers of tomatoes and bread cubes in a buttered shallow baking dish, ending with bread cubes. There should be four layers—tomatoes, then bread cubes, tomatoes again, and ending with bread cubes. Sprinkle the top layer of the bread cubes with the crumbled blue cheese and grated Parmesan cheese. Bake uncovered in a 350° oven for 30 minutes. Serves 6 to 8.

Grated Zucchini

Zucchini has become increasingly popular as a vegetable and can be served with just about anything. You can make this particular recipe for a large crowd or just for two. Vary the amount of zucchini with the number of servings you will need and adjust the recipe accordingly.

melted butter
zucchini, coarsely grated (leave skin on)
onion, grated (not too much, about 1 teaspoon per zucchini)
salt and pepper
Parmesan cheese, grated

Melt some butter in a skillet. Season the grated zucchini with the onion, salt, and pepper. Sauté lightly, just until it begins to soften. Remove from the heat. Put into a casserole, sprinkle with the grated Parmesan cheese and place under the broiler until the cheese is brown.

Breads

Refrigerator Baking Powder Biscuits

You make a batch of the mix, keep it in the refrigerator, and use it as needed.

Basic Mix:

6 cups sifted flour
4½ tablespoons baking powder
1 tablespoon salt
¾ cup butter or margarine

Sift together the flour, baking powder, and salt. Cut in the butter with a pastry blender. Put into a container and store in the refrigerator. When a fresh batch of biscuits is needed, use 2 cups of the mix and stir in ¾ to 1 cup of milk. Cut pieces of the mix on a floured board and bake in a 450° oven for 10 to 12 minutes.

Bran Muffins

More and more people are becoming aware of the importance that bran plays in our diet. Since becoming aware of this myself, I find I am making these muffins regularly. If I try to substitute bakery ones, there are always complaints. And if I am late for an early morning golf game and have a skimpy breakfast, I stick a couple of these muffins into my golf bag!

2 cups 100% bran
1 cup bran buds (or All-Bran)
1 cup boiling water
1 cup raisins
1½ cups sugar
½ cup salad oil

2 beaten eggs
2 cups buttermilk
2½ cups flour
1 teaspoon salt
2½ teaspoons baking soda

Pour the boiling water over the bran and bran buds. Fold in the raisins and let cool. In the large bowl of a mixer, cream the sugar and salad oil. Add the eggs and buttermilk. Sift the flour, salt, and soda and add to the above. Mix well. Fold in the bran and raisin mixture. Spoon into muffin tins and bake 15 to 20 minutes in a 400° oven. Makes about 2½ dozen large muffins.

Brown Bread

I am including only a few bread recipes. Who has time to bake bread during the golfing season? Here is my favorite brown bread recipe which my sister-in-law gave me twenty-four years ago.

2 cups boiling water
⅓ cup brown sugar
1 cup oatmeal
2 tablespoons butter
1 tablespoon salt
1 package dry yeast (follow directions)
⅓ cup molasses
4 to 6 cups flour

Put the 2 cups of boiling water into a large bowl. Add the brown sugar, oatmeal, butter, and salt. Let stand ½ hour. Prepare the yeast and add to the above mixture. Add the molasses. Stir in 3½ to 4 cups of the flour. Knead in the remaining flour. Knead until the dough is stiff and dry, about 10 minutes. Let rise for 3½ to 4 hours. Shape into loaves. Let rise for 1 hour. Bake in a 350° oven for 1 hour. Grease the tops of the loaves with butter while they are still warm—this gives them a nice shiny appearance.

Coffee Tin Bread

Use the one pound coffee cans with the plastic lids. This bread does not require any kneading and is really easier to make than a cake.

1 package dry yeast
½ cup warm water
¼ teaspoon ginger
1 tablespoon sugar
13 ounces evaporated milk
1 teaspoon salt
2 tablespoons salad oil
2 tablespoons sugar
4 to 4½ cups flour

In a large bowl combine the yeast, warm water, ginger, and 1 tablespoon of sugar. Let stand 15 minutes. In a large measuring cup, combine the evaporated milk, salt, salad oil, and 2 tablespoons of sugar. Stir until the sugar has dissolved, then add to the above mixture. Stir in the 4 to 4½ cups of flour. Grease well two 1 pound coffee tins. Divide the dough into two and put into the tins. Cover with the plastic lids. Let stand until the lids pop—approximately 1½ hours. Bake immediately in a 350° oven for 45 minutes.

Coffee Tin Graham Bread

*I find I have a hard time choosing a favorite between this Graham Bread and
the preceding recipe for Coffee Tin Bread. The family is split down the middle,
so I have to alternate in order to please everyone.*

2 tablespoons brown sugar
1 cup flour
1 tablespoon baking powder
2 cups Graham flour
½ teaspoon baking soda
½ teaspoon salt
⅔ cup powdered milk
1¾ cups water

Sift all the above ingredients together except the water. (The Graham flour
might be difficult to sift, so cheat a little and add it separately.) Then add the 1¾
cups water. Stir just to mix. Pour into two well greased 1 pound coffee tins,
sealed with 2 layers of foil. Bake in a 350° oven for 1½ hours. Do not peek!
Remove from the tins immediately.

Dutch Cheese Bread

Makes great toast!

1 cup milk
1 tablespoon butter
2 tablespoons sugar
2 teaspoons salt
1 teaspoon sugar

¾ cup lukewarm water
1 package dry yeast
4 to 4½ cups flour
2 cups grated Gouda cheese
cornmeal

Scald the milk. Stir in the butter, sugar, and salt. Cool to lukewarm. Mix the 1
teaspoon of sugar in the ¾ cup of lukewarm water. Sprinkle the yeast on top and
let sit for 10 minutes. Stir it down and add to the milk mixture. Mix in 2 cups of
the flour and the grated Gouda cheese. Add an additional cup of the flour and stir
well. Place the dough on a well floured surface and knead in the remaining 1 to
1½ cups of flour until the dough is smooth and elastic. Put into a well greased
bowl, turning once to grease the top. Let the dough rise for 1½ hours or until it is
double in size. Punch down and divide the dough into two. Shape into loaves
and place into greased pans which have been sprinkled with the cornmeal, or
shape into round loaves and put on greased cookie sheets which have been
sprinkled with cornmeal. There is room for two loaves on the same cookie sheet,
but only just. Let the dough rise another hour, or until doubled. Bake in the
lower third of the oven at 375° for 10 minutes, then reduce the heat and bake at
350° for an additional 35 minutes or until done.

Parmesan Fingers

Both these and the following anchovy fingers are nice to serve with soup or salad—not quite so filling as rolls. The proportions will depend on how many you are serving, so I will leave that up to you.

bread slices
melted butter
grated Parmesan cheese

Remove the crusts from the bread slices and cut the bread into fingers. Dip them lightly into melted butter and cover completely with the Parmesan cheese. Toast in a hot oven (425°) turning once so that both sides are nicely browned. This should not take longer than 10 minutes.

Anchovy Fingers

These are very nice with onion soup or Caesar salad.

8 bread slices, trimmed of crusts and cut into fingers
½ cup butter, soft
2 teaspoons red wine vinegar
2 tablespoons anchovy paste
2 teaspoons chopped parsley

Combine the above ingredients, except for the bread. Mix well. Spread this mixture on both sides of the bread fingers. Toast in a 400° oven, turning once half way through the baking time, so that both sides are golden brown. This should not take more than 10 minutes. Serve hot.

Louise's Popovers

We have these with roast beef. My 11-year-old daughter makes them for us— without any help.

3 eggs
1 cup milk
1 cup flour
½ teaspoon salt

Spray muffin tins with Pam (which makes removing the muffins so easy), or grease them with shortening. Mix the ingredients together and don't worry if it comes out a little lumpy. Fill the pans half full. Put them into a cold oven. Turn oven to 450° and bake for 30 minutes.

White Bread

This recipe comes from my dear friend Shirley Caron who is a wonderful cook. I have tried other bread recipes but have never found one my family likes as much as this one.

1¾ cups milk
2 tablespoons butter
2 tablespoons sugar
1½ teaspoons salt
1 package dry yeast (follow directions)
4 to 5 cups all purpose flour

Scald the milk in a double boiler. Pour it into a large mixing bowl and add the butter, sugar, and salt. Prepare the yeast and add to the above mixture. Stir in 3½ cups of the flour. Knead into the dough the remaining 1 to 1½ cups of flour. Knead until the dough is stiff and dry, about 10 minutes. Put into a greased bowl and let rise about 1½ hours. Punch down the dough. Knead again for only a minute, then shape into loaves. Put into greased pans and let rise for 1 hour. Bake in a 375° oven for 10 minutes, then reduce the heat and bake at 350° for 35 minutes or until cooked. To test if the bread is done, tap the top of the loaf—if it sounds hollow, it is done.

White Muffins

I make these muffins quite frequently, as they take very little time to assemble. I make them in the large sized muffin tins—this recipe makes eight generous muffins. Be sure to loosen the muffins and remove them from the pan once they are cooked if you like a crisp outside—a nice contrast to the lovely fluffy inside. These freeze very well.

2 cups flour
¼ cup sugar
¾ teaspoon salt
3 teaspoons baking powder
1 egg, unbeaten
1 cup milk
¼ cup melted margarine

Sift together into a bowl the flour, sugar, salt, and baking powder. Add the egg, milk, and margarine. Mix only until all the flour has been absorbed. Use a large wire whisk instead of getting out a mixer for such a little job. Grease some muffin tins and fill them ⅔ full. Sprinkle the tops with a mixture of cinnamon and sugar. (Keep a shaker of this mixture on the shelf—it is often useful.) Bake in a 425° oven for 20 minutes.

Mother's Yorkshire Pudding

I don't think we ever had roast beef without Yorkshire pudding when I was growing up. I am always so surprised when some people don't even know what it is.

2 or 3 tablespoons drippings from the roast
¾ cup plus 2 tablespoons flour
½ teaspoon salt
2 eggs
½ cup milk
½ cup water

Put the fat drippings from the roast into an 8 inch square pan. Put into a 400° oven and when hot, pour in the rest of the ingredients which have been mixed together. Don't worry if it is a little lumpy. Bake in the 400° oven for 30 to 40 minutes. Don't at any time lower the heat. It will puff up beautifully if directions are followed. This doubles well. Just use a larger pan. Serves 6.

Zucchini Bread

2 cups sugar
1 cup oil
3 eggs
3 cups flour
1 teaspoon salt
1 teaspoon baking powder

1 teaspoon cinnamon
½ cup milk
1 teaspoon vanilla
⅔ cup chopped nuts
2 cups zucchini, peeled and grated

Cream the sugar and oil. Add the eggs, one at a time. Sift the flour, salt, baking powder, and cinnamon, and add to the first mixture alternately with the milk. Add the vanilla. Fold in the nuts and zucchini. Put into 2 loaf pans and bake for 1 hour in a 350° oven or until done.

Cakes and Frostings

CAKES

Banana Cake

Moist and delicious.

4 tablespoons butter
1½ cups sugar
3 eggs
2 bananas, mashed
1¾ cups flour

1 teaspoon baking soda
½ teaspoon baking powder
½ teaspoon salt
½ cup sour cream
1 teaspoon vanilla

Cream the butter and sugar. Add the eggs one at a time, beating after each addition. Add the mashed bananas. Sift the dry ingredients together and add to the above mixture alternately with the sour cream. Add the vanilla. Bake in a 9 inch square pan at 350° for 40 minutes or until done. Sprinkle with icing sugar or frost with a white icing.

Carrot Cake

A lovely moist cake. Can be made in a tube pan.

2 cups sugar
1¼ cups salad oil
2 cups flour
½ teaspoon salt

2 teaspoons cinnamon
1¾ teaspoons soda
4 eggs
3 cups grated carrots

Cream the sugar and oil. Combine the dry ingredients and add to the creamed mixture. Add the eggs one at a time, beating well after each addition. Stir in the carrots. Pour the batter into three 9 inch round layer pans. Bake in a 350° oven for 30 minutes or until the cake springs back when touched lightly in the center.

Icing for Carrot Cake:

8 ounces cream cheese, softened
1 package icing sugar (1 pound)
¼ cup butter, softened

1 cup chopped pecans
1 cup flaked coconut
1 teaspoon vanilla

Mix together well the ingredients and spread between layers of the cooled cake.

Marion's Chocolate Cake

This is a heavy, moist cake which is even better the day after you bake it—it stays moist for as long as the cake lasts!

¼ cup melted shortening
¼ cup cocoa
½ cup hot water
½ cup sour milk (1 teaspoon vinegar to fresh milk will make it sour)

1 egg, beaten into sour milk
1 cup flour
1 teaspoon baking soda
pinch of salt
1 teaspoon vanilla
1 cup white sugar

Put all the ingredients into a bowl in the order given above. Beat with a mixer until smooth. Bake in an 8 inch square pan in a 350° oven for 25 to 30 minutes. Double the recipe for a layer cake and frost with either one of the chocolate frostings in the index.

Mother's Light Fruitcake

4 cups light raisins
1 cup glazed red cherries
1 cup glazed green cherries
½ pound cut glazed fruit
4 glazed pineapple rings
⅓ cup brandy or rum
1 cup butter
1 cup white sugar

4 eggs
2½ cups flour
2 teaspoons baking powder
1 teaspoon nutmeg
1 teaspoon salt
1 cup pineapple juice
1 cup pecans (optional)

The night before, cut up all the fruit and put with the raisins into a large bowl. Pour over the fruit about ⅓ cup of brandy or rum. The next day, cream the butter and sugar. Beat in the eggs, one at a time. Sift together the dry ingredients and add alternately with the pineapple juice to the creamed mixture. Combine with the cut up fruit and raisins. Use a large round fruitcake pan lined with greased brown paper, and bake it in a very slow oven, starting at 300° for ½ hour and reducing the heat to 275° for an additional 4 to 5 hours. (Test the center with a toothpick.) Put a pan of hot water into the bottom of the oven, as this keeps the cake more moist. This cake could also be baked in a tube pan—just reduce the baking time.

Jelly Roll

4 eggs
¾ cup sugar
¾ cup flour
1 teaspoon baking powder
¼ teaspoon salt
1 teaspoon vanilla

Line a jelly roll pan (cookie sheet with sides) with waxed paper. Have the eggs at room temperature. Beat the eggs for 10 minutes adding the sugar very gradually. Sift the rest of the dry ingredients together, and with a mixer at its lowest speed, fold them into the egg/sugar mixture. Add the vanilla. Bake 13 minutes in a 400° oven. While the cake bakes, lay out a kitchen towel and sprinkle it with icing sugar. When the cake is done, invert it quickly. Peel off the paper and roll the cake up in the towel. Let it cool on a rack. Spread with tart jam.

Mayonnaise Spice Cake

1 cup raisins (more if desired)
1 teaspoon cinnamon
½ teaspoon allspice
1 teaspoon mace
1 teaspoon baking soda
1 cup boiling water

Mix the above ingredients together and let them sit while mixing the following:

1 cup sugar
1 cup mayonnaise
1 teaspoon salt
2 cups flour

Add these ingredients to the first mixture. Put into a greased and floured 9 inch square pan and bake in a 350° oven for 40 minutes or until done.

Bill's Mom's Orange Date Nut Cake

3½ cups flour
1¼ teaspoons baking soda
1 teaspoon salt
1 cup butter
2 cups sugar
4 eggs

1¼ cups buttermilk
1 cup walnuts, chopped
1 cup dates, chopped
1 tablespoon grated orange rind
1 teaspoon lemon extract
1 teaspoon vanilla

Sift and measure the flour. Resift with the baking soda and salt. Cream the butter and gradually add the sugar. Cream until light. Add the eggs one at a time, beating well after each addition. Add the buttermilk and flour alternately. Stir in the nuts, dates, orange rind, and extracts. Pour into a well greased and floured tube pan and bake for 1¼ hours in a 350° oven. Leave the cake in the pan and while hot, pour on the orange glaze after making holes in the cake with an ice pick to let the glaze seep through. Do not remove from the pan until the cake is cold.

Orange Glaze:

½ cup orange juice
1 cup sugar
1 tablespoon orange rind

Combine the ingredients in a saucepan and heat to just below boiling, stirring until the sugar is dissolved.

Orange Sour Cream Cake

Simple and super.

1 teaspoon baking soda
2 cups sour cream
1 box yellow cake mix
3 eggs
grated rind of two oranges (save 1 teaspoon for icing)

Stir the baking soda into the sour cream. Empty the cake mix into a large bowl. Add the eggs, sour cream mixture, and grated orange rind. Use an electric mixer and beat at medium speed for a full 5 minutes. Empty into a greased and floured 10 inch angel food pan. Bake in a 350° oven for 45 to 50 minutes. Frost with orange butter cream icing.

Orange Butter Cream Icing:

3 tablespoons butter
1 teaspoon grated orange rind
¼ teaspoon salt
2½ cups icing sugar
4 tablespoons cream
1 teaspoon orange extract

Blend the butter, orange rind, and salt. Add the icing sugar gradually, ½ cup at a time. Add the cream and orange extract, and with an electric mixer, beat on high speed until the icing is nice and creamy.

Prune Cake

1½ cups sugar	1 cup nuts
1 cup oil	1 teaspoon salt
3 eggs	1 teaspoon nutmeg
1 teaspoon baking soda	1 teaspoon cinnamon
1 cup buttermilk	1 cup chopped, cooked prunes
2 cups flour	

Cream the sugar and oil. Beat in the eggs one at a time. Dissolve the baking soda into the buttermilk and add it to the sugar/egg mixture alternately with the sifted dry ingredients. Pour the batter into a 13 by 9 inch oblong greased and floured baking dish. Bake in a 325° oven for about 40 minutes or until done. Pour hot syrup over the cake while it is still warm.

Hot Syrup for Prune Cake:

1 cup sugar	¼ cup butter
½ cup buttermilk	1 teaspoon corn syrup
½ teaspoon soda	1 teaspoon vanilla

Bring these ingredients to a boil and cook for about 5 minutes.

Sherry Cake

1 package Duncan Hines yellow cake mix
1 package instant vanilla pudding (3¼ ounce size)
4 eggs
¾ cup oil
¾ cup sherry
1 teaspoon nutmeg

Place all the ingredients into a bowl. Beat for 5 minutes on the medium speed of an electric mixer. Grease and flour a 10 inch tube pan, pour in the batter and bake for 45 minutes in a 350° oven.

FROSTINGS

Easy Butterscotch Frosting

Nice on butterscotch squares (see index).

6 tablespoons butter
¾ cup brown sugar, packed
6 tablespoons light cream
2 cups icing sugar
½ teaspoon vanilla

Heat the butter, brown sugar, and cream slowly until the sugar is dissolved, stirring constantly. Boil for 1 minute. Remove from the heat and add the icing sugar and vanilla. Beat until cool, about 5 minutes. Add milk if the frosting is too thick, or more icing sugar if it is too thin.

Chocolate Frosting #1

This frosting is light in color which contrasts nicely with a dark chocolate cake. I have to keep alternating between this and the following chocolate frosting (#2) because the men in the family prefer #1 and we gals think we prefer #2!

½ pound butter (not margarine)
2 cups icing sugar
3 tablespoons Nestlé's Quick
2 ounces rum
1 teaspoon instant coffee

Beat together well all the ingredients. This is sufficient for a two layer cake—the top, sides, and between layers.

Chocolate Frosting #2

⅓ cup butter
2 squares bitter chocolate
1 cup icing sugar
¼ cup canned milk
pinch of salt
1 teaspoon vanilla
1 egg unbeaten

Melt the butter and chocolate in a double boiler. Combine in a mixing bowl the rest of the ingredients. Add this mixture to the chocolate mixture and place the pan into ice water. Beat until fluffy. Frosting may be kept in the refrigerator. Double the ingredients for a two layer cake.

Honey Icing

This is quite similar to a boiled icing. I spoke to a young woman recently who told me she really didn't like any desserts that had sugar in them. This icing would be great for her, but I haven't come up with a cake she could put under it.

1 egg white
1 cup liquid honey
pinch of salt
½ teaspoon vanilla

With an electric mixer, beat the egg white, honey, and salt together at high speed until the icing stands up in peaks. This will take about 7 to 10 minutes. Add the vanilla slowly and continue to beat only until the vanilla is absorbed. Serve on anything for which a boiled icing is used.

Orange Butter Cream Icing

3 tablespoons butter
1 teaspoon grated orange rind
¼ teaspoon salt
2½ cups icing sugar
4 tablespoons cream
1 teaspoon orange extract

Blend together the butter, orange rind, and salt. Add the icing sugar gradually, ½ cup at a time. Add the cream and extract and beat with an electric mixer on high speed until the icing is nice and creamy.

Cookies and Squares

Butterscotch Squares

1 cup brown sugar
½ cup butter
1 egg
1 cup flour

1 cup shredded coconut
2 teaspoons baking powder
pinch of salt
½ teaspoon vanilla

Melt the sugar and butter in a saucepan. Add the egg, dry ingredients, and coconut. Bake in an 8 inch square pan in a 350° oven for 25 minutes. Frost with Butterscotch Frosting (see index).

Chocolate Brownies

2 squares chocolate
½ cup butter
2 eggs
4 tablespoons cold water
1 cup sugar
¾ cup flour

½ teaspoon baking powder
½ teaspoon salt
1 teaspoon vanilla
1 cup walnuts (cut up and floured)

Melt together and cool the chocolate and butter. In a separate bowl, beat the 2 eggs well and add the rest of the ingredients. Then add the melted chocolate and butter mixture. Bake in a 350° oven for about 30 minutes.

Chocolate Chip Squares

Gooey and yummy!

11 double graham wafers, crushed
½ cup desiccated coconut
½ package chocolate chips (6 ounce size)
1 teaspoon vanilla
1 teaspoon baking powder
pinch of salt
1 tin Eagle brand milk

Mix together the ingredients in the order given. Put into a well greased 8 inch square pan. Bake in a 375° oven for 20 minutes.

Ice Box Cookies

¾ cup butter
1 cup dark brown sugar
1 egg
2 cups flour

½ teaspoon baking soda
½ teaspoon cream of tartar
½ teaspoon vanilla
1 cup chopped walnuts, optional

Cream the butter and sugar. Add the egg, flour, baking soda, cream of tartar, and vanilla. Add 1 cup of chopped walnuts at this time, if desired. Shape into an oblong and put into the refrigerator. (An empty foil or plastic wrap box lined with waxed paper makes a good container for this cookie dough.) Slice thinly when ready to bake. Bake in a 350° oven for 10 to 15 minutes.

Marshmallow Squares

30 graham wafers, crushed (about 1½ cups crumbs)
1 can Eagle brand milk
2 full cups miniature marshmallows
1 cup desiccated coconut
16 glazed cherries, chopped

Sprinkle some of the graham wafer crumbs into the bottom of a greased 8 inch square pan. Save a few crumbs for the top. Mix together the remaining crumbs and all the other ingredients and press into a pan. Sprinkle the remaining crumbs on top. Let stand 24 hours in a cool place.

Meringues

This is one of the children's favorite desserts. They like the meringues best just put together (upright) with either vanilla or butterscotch ripple ice cream in between and whipped cream on top.

1 teaspoon vanilla
1 teaspoon vinegar
1 teaspoon water
1 cup berry sugar
½ teaspoon baking powder
⅛ teaspoon salt
3 or 4 egg whites (4 is best but 3 will do)

Combine the vanilla, vinegar, and water in a small cup. Mix the sugar, baking powder, and salt together. Beat the egg whites until stiff. Add to the egg whites the sugar mixture, about 1 teaspoon at a time, alternately with ½ teaspoon of the combined liquids. When the mixture is stiff, place spoonfuls of it (about 2½ inches in diameter) on a lightly greased cookie sheet and shape the meringues with a heavy edge. Bake in a very slow oven (225° to 275°) for 1½ to 2 hours. Cool before removing from the pan.

Oatmeal Cookies

Always a favorite.

1 cup white sugar
½ cup brown sugar
1 cup shortening (½ cup lard and ½ cup margarine if desired)
1 egg
1½ cups flour
pinch of salt
1 teaspoon baking soda
1 teaspoon baking powder
1¼ cup rolled oats
¾ cup flaked coconut

Cream the shortening with the sugar. Add the egg and beat well. Sift the flour, salt, baking soda, and baking powder together, and add to the creamed mixture. Add the rolled oats and coconut, and blend well. Onto a greased cookie sheet, drop the batter by the teaspoon and flatten with a fork dipped into water. Bake in a 350° oven for 8 to 10 minutes.

Orange Coconut Chews

¼ cup butter
1 cup brown sugar
1 egg
1 teaspoon vanilla
2 teaspoons grated orange rind

½ cup all purpose flour
½ teaspoon salt
1 teaspoon baking powder
1 cup shredded coconut
1 cup chopped dates

Melt the butter. Remove it from the heat and stir in the brown sugar. Blend in the egg, vanilla, and orange rind. Mix together the flour, salt, and baking powder. Stir this into the butter mixture. Stir in the coconut and dates. Spread in a greased 7 by 11 inch pan. Bake for 30 minutes in a 350° oven. When cool, cut into squares. Ice with a thin icing if desired.

Peanut Butter Balls

Children love these. Put a few into your golf bag for a nutritious snack.

1 cup corn syrup
½ cup white sugar
pinch of salt
1 teaspoon vanilla
1 cup peanut butter
2 cups slightly crushed cornflakes
2 cups Rice Krispies

Bring the corn syrup and sugar to a boil. Mix in the rest of the ingredients and roll into balls—they will roll more easily if your hands are buttered.

Flossie's Shortbread Cookies

Not quite as easy as the following recipe for shortbread cookies which are dropped from a teaspoon, but I have been making these at Christmas-time for twenty-three years. The recipe was given to me by a girl who worked for my mother when I was very young, and I thought she made the best cookies in the whole world.

½ cup cornstarch
½ cup icing sugar
1 cup flour
1 cup butter

Mix together well the ingredients. Roll out on a lightly floured surface and cut with a very small cookie cutter. Don't roll too thinly. Bake in a 300° oven until done—15 to 20 minutes depending on the thickness of the cookies.

Mrs. Tandy's Whipped Shortbread Cookies

If I have to send cookies to school for anything—a bake sale, party, or whatever—I send these. This recipe makes a huge quantity and the children love them. The first time I sent these cookies to a bake sale at school, the teachers bought them to have with their tea. They sent notes home asking for the recipe! These cookies literally melt in your mouth.

1 pound margarine (don't substitute butter or they will be too short)
1 cup icing sugar
½ cup cornstarch
3 cups flour
1 teaspoon vanilla
few maraschino cherries, but in small pieces

Cream the margarine. Add the sugar, cornstarch, and flour in that order. Then add the vanilla. Beat the mixture until it is whipped like cream. Drop the batter a teaspoon at a time onto a cookie sheet. Decorate each with a piece of maraschino cherry. Bake in a 350° oven for about 12 minutes. They spread only a wee bit.

Pies and Pastries

Chess Pie

A custard type pie with a wonderfully delicate flavor.

1¼ sticks butter or margarine
1½ cups sugar
1 teaspoon flour
¼ teaspoon salt
5 egg yolks
1 cup evaporated milk
1½ teaspoons vanilla
10 inch unbaked pie shell
5 egg whites
¼ teaspoon cream of tartar
½ cup sugar

Cream the butter. Add the sugar and cream well. Add the flour, salt, and egg yolks, and cream together. Add the milk and beat. (Don't be alarmed if the mixture appears curdled.) Add the vanilla. Beat again and pour into the unbaked pie shell. Bake for 10 minutes in a 400° oven, then reduce heat to 300° and bake for an additional 30 to 40 minutes, until brown on top. Remove from the oven and cool the pie slightly while making the meringue.

Meringue:

Beat the 5 egg whites with the cream of tartar until frothy. Beat in the sugar a little at a time. Beat until stiff. Cover the pie, spreading well to the edges, so as to seal the filling. Bake an additional 10 minutes.

Eggnog Pie

A Christmas-time special pie.

1 tablespoon gelatin
¼ cup cold water
4 egg yolks
½ cup sugar
½ teaspoon salt
½ cup hot water
4 egg whites
¼ cup sugar
1½ tablespoons rum
1 baked pie shell
1 cup cream, whipped
nutmeg

Soak the gelatin in ¼ cup of cold water for 5 minutes. Beat the egg yolks and add the ½ cup of sugar, the salt, and hot water. Put into a double boiler and cook until the mixture is of custard consistency, stirring constantly. Remove from the heat and add the gelatin. Stir until the gelatin is dissolved. Beat the egg whites until stiff, adding the ¼ cup of sugar gradually. Fold into the yolk mixture along with the 1½ tablespoons of rum. Fill the baked pie shell and put into the refrigerator to set. Spread with a thin layer of whipped cream and a light sprinkling of nutmeg before serving.

Pastry Kuchen

2 cups sifted enriched flour
½ pound softened butter
½ pint sour cream
1 large package chocolate chips
1 tablespoon butter
2 tablespoons milk
chopped nuts

Mix the flour and butter together with a fork until pieces of the mixture crumble to the size of a pea. Add the sour cream and mix well. Divide into two balls. Wrap each ball in waxed paper and refrigerate overnight. The next day, melt 1 large package of chocolate chips in the top of a double boiler. Add the butter and 2 tablespoons of milk. Take 1 ball of dough out of the refrigerator and roll it, working quickly, to about a 10 by 15 inch size. Spread half of the chocolate mixture over the dough and sprinkle it with the chopped nuts. Roll up the dough like a jelly roll, pinching the ends so that the filling does not escape. Repeat with the second ball. Place them on a cookie sheet and bake in a 325° oven for about 1 hour. Watch the pastry carefully.

Lemon Butter Filling for Small Tarts

This is an old recipe of my mother's. When I was a new bride, I didn't have any trouble with her recipes which called for butter the size of an egg—I simply went to the refrigerator, got an egg, and cut the butter around it. The recipes which asked for 'enough' flour, or to add flour until it 'feels right', were the ones which sent me running for the phone. But we lived 350 miles away from my mother, so my husband thought that it would be a good idea if I finally bought a proper cookbook!

2 cups white sugar
4 eggs
3 lemons—juice of 3, rind of 1
butter, the size of an egg

Cream the sugar and eggs. Add the juice of the 3 lemons and the rind of 1. Mix them well and add the butter. Cook,* stirring constantly until thick. Use in cooked tart shells or meringue shells. This filling keeps very well in the refrigerator.

*Note: Use top of double boiler.

Lemon Tart Filling made with Lemonade

This is the tart filling I make if I happen to be in need of egg whites. My children adore meringues and angel food cake, so I often look for recipes using only yolks.

¼ pound butter
⅔ cup sugar
grated rind of 1 lemon
1 small can frozen lemonade concentrate
6 egg yolks, beaten slightly

Melt the butter in the top of a double boiler. Add the ⅔ cup of sugar and mix well. Add the lemon rind. Stir in the lemonade concentrate and egg yolks. Cook over hot water, stirring constantly until the mixture is thick and smooth.

Pastry for Small Tarts

These are both excellent crusts. The first one I use for fillings which are to be cooked with the crust, and the second one is baked first, then filled with a cooked filling.

#1 Cream Cheese Pastry:

3 ounces cream cheese
½ cup butter or margarine
1 cup sifted all purpose flour

Soften the cream cheese and butter. Blend them together. Stir in the flour. Chill for at least 1 hour. Shape into 2 dozen 1 inch balls. Place them into tiny ungreased muffin tins, pressing the dough evenly on the bottom and sides. Add any uncooked filling and bake.

#2 Shortbread Pastry:

1 cup butter
½ cup icing sugar
pinch of salt
2 cups flour
2 teaspoons cornstarch

Blend together the butter and sugar. Add the rest of the ingredients. Knead until smooth. Roll into small balls and press into tart pans. Bake in a 300° oven for 20 minutes.

Pecan Pie

Sinful, but what the heck!

3 eggs
⅔ cup white sugar
⅓ teaspoon salt
⅓ cup melted butter
1 cup dark Karo syrup (corn syrup)
1 cup pecan halves
1 teaspoon vanilla
1 unbaked 9 inch pastry shell

Beat together all the ingredients except the pecans and vanilla. Then mix in the pecan halves and vanilla. Fill the pastry shell. Bake in a 350° oven for 40 to 50 minutes or until a knife inserted in the middle comes out clean. Serve whipped cream on the side in case not everyone wants it on the pie.

Pecan Filling for Small Tarts

1 egg
¾ cup brown sugar
1 tablespoon butter or margarine
1 teaspoon vanilla
dash of salt
small package of pecans

Beat together until smooth all the ingredients except the pecans. Put the pecans into the bottom of small unbaked tart shells, add the filling, and bake for 25 minutes. Cool before removing the tarts from their pans.

Rhubarb Cream Pie

This pie needs no top crust, no whipping cream, no meringue on top. It is perfect just by itself.

2 tablespoons butter
1½ cups sugar
2 eggs, beaten
2 rounded tablespoons flour
3 cups cut up rhubarb
9 inch unbaked pie shell

Cream together the butter and sugar. Add the beaten eggs. Mix in the flour. Fold in the rhubarb. Fill the unbaked pie shell and bake in a 400° oven for 10 minutes. Reduce the heat and bake 40 to 45 minutes longer or until the filling has formed a top crust.

Corrine's Strawberry Pie

This recipe comes from a friend of my mother's and it is SO good. Thank you Corrine!

9 inch baked pastry shell
2 boxes fresh strawberries
1 cup water
½ cup sugar
4 teaspoons cornstarch
bit of red food coloring
whipped cream

Line the cooked pastry shell with the whole strawberries, about 3 layers. Crush 1 large cup of the strawberries. Combine it with 1 cup of water and boil for 3 minutes, then strain. To the strained juice add the ½ cup of sugar and 4 teaspoons cornstarch mixed with a little of the juice to make a paste. Cook and stir until thick and clear. Tint with a bit of the red food coloring. Cool slightly and spoon over the berries in the pie shell. Refrigerate until serving time. Spread whipped cream over top before serving.

Desserts

Almond Crisps

Once you master the art of removing these from the pan—like golf, it is just timing—you will be serving them at every dinner party.

¼ cup flour
¼ teaspoon salt
½ cup sugar
1 cup sliced almonds
½ cup butter
2 tablespoons whipping cream

Sift the flour, measure it, then sift it again with the salt and sugar into a small saucepan. Add the almonds, butter, and cream. Cook over low heat until the mixture bubbles, about 5 minutes. Remove from the heat and stir briskly for 30 seconds. Drop by the teaspoon onto a baking sheet and bake for about 5 minutes in a 375° oven. It is very important to roll these cookies at just the right moment, as they harden very quickly and tear apart if they are too hot. Try them one at a time at first until getting the feel of it. Bake no more than 4 at a time as they spread a great deal. Have 4 wooden spoons handy—the cookies will be rolled around their handles as is done with brandy snaps. Store the cookies in a cool dry place until they are to be filled with whipped cream. Don't fill them too far ahead of time or they will soften. Just before serving, fill them with whipped cream—a pastry bag is useful for this. Serve two per person and provide a dessert fork and spoon so the guests can handle the crisps easily. Also try making flat ones and sandwiching them with ice cream.

Sherry Almond Pudding

Ethereal is the only way to describe this dessert.

2 tablespoons unflavored gelatin	6 egg whites
½ cup cold water	1½ cups sugar
1 cup hot water	1 cup heavy cream, whipped
⅓ cup sherry	1 cup almonds, shredded
½ teaspoon almond extract	extra shredded almonds and toasted
¼ teaspoon salt	coconut for garnish

Soak the gelatin in cold water. Dissolve it in hot water and cool. Add the sherry, almond extract, and salt. When the mixture begins to thicken, beat until frothy. Beat the egg whites until stiff. Fold the egg whites, sugar, and whipped cream into the gelatin mixture. Chill until almost firm. Pour into a 3 quart melon mold, alternating the mixture with 1 cup of almonds. Chill at least 4 hours. Unmold and garnish with almonds and coconut. Serve with the Sherry Custard Sauce (recipe following). Serves 10.

Sherry Custard Sauce:

6 egg yolks	2 cups scalded milk
¼ cup sugar	¼ cup sherry
2 tablespoons flour	1 cup cream, whipped

Beat the egg yolks thoroughly. Mix in the sugar and flour. Gradually stir in the scalded milk. Cook over low heat until thickened, stirring constantly. Cool. Add the ¼ cup sherry. Chill. This recipe can be made the day before, up to this point. When ready to serve, fold in the whipped cream.

Cheesecake

Crust:

2 cups graham cracker crumbs (scant)
¼ stick butter
2 tablespoons brown sugar

Combine these ingredients and press into a greased 10 inch tube cake spring form pan. Bake 10 minutes in a 350° oven. Cool.

Filling:

5 eggs, large size
24 ounces cream cheese (softened)
1 cup sugar
2 teaspoons fresh lemon juice
1 teaspoon vanilla

Preheat the oven to 350°. Beat the eggs until light and combine with the cream cheese. Blend well. Add the sugar, lemon juice, and vanilla. Beat until smooth. Pour onto the crust and bake in a 350° oven for 30 minutes or until just firm.

Topping:

Let the cheesecake stand at room temperature for 20 minutes, then pour on the following ingredients which have been mixed together:

1 cup sour cream
¼ cup sugar
1 teaspoon vanilla

Return the cheesecake to the oven and bake an additional 5 minutes. When it cools, spread it with a can of blueberry or cherry pie filling or the following pineapple glaze (although it doesn't really need anything).

Pineapple Glaze:

1 small can crushed pineapple
2 tablespoons sugar
1 tablespoon cornstarch

Cook over low heat until thick. Cool and spread carefully on top of the cheesecake. Serves 10.

Annie's Cheesecake

Crust:

24 graham crackers, crushed
1 teaspoon cinnamon
½ cup sugar
¼ cup melted butter

Combine the above ingredients and press into the bottom of a greased 8 inch square cake pan. Bake 10 minutes in a 350° oven. Cool.

Filling:

3 eggs
8 ounces cream cheese, softened
½ cup sugar
2 cups cottage cheese
2 teaspoons vanilla
1 cup crushed pineapple, well drained
½ cup coconut (fresh if possible)

Beat the eggs until light. Combine them with the cream cheese and blend well. Add the sugar, cottage cheese, vanilla, pineapple, and coconut. Mix well and pour over the graham cracker crust. Bake in a 375° oven for 30 minutes. Cool. Serves 8.

THAT'S WHAT I'LL SERVE TONIGHT, MAUDE— CHINESE BEEF AND GREENS!!

No-Bake Cheesecake

Crust:

2 cups graham cracker crumbs
¼ pound margarine
1 teaspoon vanilla
1 tablespoon brown sugar

Mix the ingredients together and pack into the bottom of two 8 inch pie plates or one 13 by 9 inch pan. Add 1 teaspoon or more of water if the crust does not pack.

Filling:

2 envelopes Dream Whip
1 cup milk
8 ounces cream cheese
½ cup sugar
1 can cherry pie filling

Whip the Dream Whip and milk until thick. In another bowl mix the cream cheese and sugar and beat well. Spoon this mixture into the Dream Whip and combine thoroughly. Pour over the graham cracker crust. Put the cheesecake into the freezer to firm it before attempting to put the topping on—it is then much easier to spread. Spread the pie filling over top. Serves 8 to 10.

Chocolate Mousse

*If you are the type who is turned off by any recipe containing Dream Whip,
don't be too hasty in passing over this one. If you entertain large crowds, this
recipe doubles, triples, etc. beautifully, and we golfers don't have a lot of time
to spend in the kitchen! I am going to give you the recipe for 6, then just below
it the recipe for 20, because I find it very handy to have it written in front of
me. Sometimes trying to multiply something '4 times' in your head works only
if you are not doing too many other things at the same time (which might
happen if you're having 20 guests for dinner the following night). This recipe is
so 'cinchy', yet it tastes as though you spent hours preparing it.*

For 6 servings:

1 package chocolate Whip and Chill
¼ cup rum
¼ cup water
1½ teaspoons Camp coffee (it comes in a bottle, but if it can't be found at the
    supermarket, just liquify some instant coffee, making sure it is very strong)
1 package Dream Whip

Make the Whip and Chill according to the directions on the package, but instead
of the water called for in the recipe, use the rum, water, and coffee. To this
mixture, fold in the Dream Whip which has been prepared according to the
instructions on the package. Chill.

For 20 servings:

4 packages chocolate Whip and Chill
2 cups cold milk
1 cup rum
1 cup water
5 teaspoons Camp coffee
4 packages Dream Whip
2 cups cold milk
2 teaspoons vanilla

Use a punch bowl to serve this. Make sure the bowls in which the Whip and
Chill and Dream Whip are being prepared are chilled and large enough, as the
mixtures will increase in volume. Follow the instructions in the above recipe,
only use these quantities.

Quick Blender Chocolate Mousse

Chocolate Mousse is a very popular dessert. This one is particularly easy and quick to prepare.

6 ounces chocolate chips
2 eggs
3 tablespoons very strong hot coffee
¾ cup scalded milk (just below boiling point)
1 to 2 tablespoons rum

Put all the ingredients into a blender in the order listed. Blend at high speed for about 2 minutes. Pour into individual pots au crème or demitasse cups. Serves 4.

Crème Brûlée

This is high on the list of all-time favorites with my family. It is often referred to as burnt cream, but please don't burn it.

2 cups light cream
1 tablespoon sugar
4 egg yolks
1 teaspoon vanilla
light brown sugar

Heat the cream in a double boiler until hot but not scalding. Add the 1 tablespoon of sugar and stir until dissolved. Beat the egg yolks until light. Add them with the vanilla to the cream. (Remember to add a little of the hot mixture to the egg yolks first so they don't curdle.) Mix well and pour into a shallow baking dish. Have a dish large enough so that the custard is about 1½ inches deep. Place the dish into hot water and bake in a 325° oven until set, about 50 to 60 minutes. Cool and place the dish into the refrigerator for several hours to chill thoroughly. Remove from the refrigerator and cover the entire surface with ⅛ inch of sifted light brown sugar. Place the dish under the broiler and watch very carefully so that it does not burn. When the surface is glazed, remove, cool, and place the dish back into the refrigerator to cool thoroughly. Serves 4.

White Grapes with Sour Cream

Couldn't be easier or more delicious.

white grapes
brown sugar
sour cream

The amounts will depend on how many people are being served. Put a layer of grapes into the bottom of a bowl. Sprinkle brown sugar over them. Add a layer of sour cream. Repeat the layers and let stand for 4 hours in the refrigerator. This recipe can be made the night before.

Ice Cream Pecan Balls

1 pint vanilla ice cream
1 cup toasted pecans, chopped
butterscotch sauce (see index)

Scoop the ice cream into balls then roll them in the pecans. Keep in a refrigerator tray in the freezer until ready to use. Before serving, put the balls into dishes and cover with the butterscotch sauce.

Lemon Sherry Mold

6 eggs, separated
1 cup sugar
2 envelopes gelatin
¾ cup sherry
1 lemon, juice and grated rind

Beat the egg yolks well. Add the sugar and continue beating very well, until light. Soak the gelatin in the sherry for 5 minutes. Dissolve the gelatin over hot water. Add the lemon rind and juice to the egg yolk mixture. Gradually add the dissolved gelatin, beating until well mixed. Beat the egg whites until stiff and fold them into the egg yolk and gelatin mixture. Pour into a melon mold and refrigerate. Serve with the following Sherry Custard Sauce. Serves 8 to 10.

Sherry Custard Sauce:

3 eggs yolks
2 tablespoons sugar
1 tablespoon flour
1 cup milk, scalded
2 tablespoons sherry
½ cup cream, whipped

Beat the egg yolks thoroughly. Mix in the sugar and flour. Gradually stir in the scalded milk. Cook over a low heat until thickened, stirring constantly. Cool. Add the sherry. Chill. Fold in the whipped cream.

Frozen Lemon Soufflé

1 envelope gelatin	⅔ cup lemon juice
¼ cup cold water	1 tablespoon grated lemon rind
6 egg yolks	4 egg whites
1 cup sugar	1½ cups whipping cream

Soften the gelatin in the cold water. Beat the egg yolks into the sugar until thick and light. Stir in the lemon juice. Cook over low heat, beating constantly until thick but do not let it boil. Mix in the gelatin until dissolved. Add the lemon rind. Remove from the heat and cool. Stir occasionally. Beat the egg whites until stiff but not dry, and fold into the lemon mixture. Whip the cream and fold it in. Carefully pour into a shallow spring form pan. Put into the freezer. Before serving, remove from the freezer about ½ hour ahead of time—this will make for easier slicing. Serves 10.

Meringue Party Dessert

	Meringues:	
meringues	6 egg whites (large)	2 teaspoons vinegar
ice cream, 1 quart	2 cups berry sugar	2 teaspoons water
whipped cream, 1 pint	2 teaspoons vanilla	1 teaspoon baking powder
		¼ teaspoon salt

Combine vanilla, vinegar and water in a small cup. Mix sugar, baking powder and salt together. Beat the egg whites until stiff. Add to the egg whites—the sugar mixture, about 1 teaspoon at a time alternately with ½ teaspoon of the combined liquids. When this has been added, place spoonfuls on lightly greased cookie sheets, or line cookie sheets with waxed paper, making sure the shiny side is up, and shape the meringues with a slightly heavy edge. Make slightly larger ones for the bottom layer, medium sized ones for middle layer and smaller ones for the top (roughly 4½″, 3½″ and 2½″).

Bake in a slow oven 225 to 250 degrees for 1½ to 2 hours. What you are doing is drying them out rather than 'cooking' them.

To assemble Dessert:

On a large cake plate or silver tray place the first layer of meringues in a circle, with one in the center (5 or 6 meringues). With a serving spoon, rather than an ice cream scoop (meringues will sit better) cover this layer well with ice cream, cover ice cream layer with ½ the whipped cream. Place 2nd layer of meringues on top of whipped cream, a smaller circle this time. Cover with ice cream. Cover ice cream with remaining whipped cream. Top with the smaller meringues, making a still smaller circle. It is best to make this ahead and store in freezer unless you have an extra pair of hands in the kitchen, but remove from freezer about 20 minutes before you plan to serve it.

This is particularly spectacular when served at a birthday party. Place candles in the three layers of meringues, but be sure to start lighting candles at the top of the cake first!

Orange Bavarian Cream

1 envelope gelatin
1¼ cups fresh orange juice
1 tablespoon fresh lemon juice
½ cup sugar
1 tablespoon grated orange rind
1 cup heavy cream, whipped

Soak the gelatin in ¼ cup of the orange juice for 5 minutes. Mix together the gelatin, remaining orange juice, lemon juice, sugar, and orange rind. Bring to a boil, stirring until the gelatin is dissolved. Beat until fluffy. Fold in the whipped cream. Put into a mold or serving dish and chill. Serves 4.

Orange Slices in Curaçao

Orange slices are more delicious when served in the following manner.

6 oranges
¼ cup Curaçao
½ cup freshly grated coconut

Peel and slice the oranges. Marinate them in the Curaçao overnight in the refrigerator. Arrange the orange slices in individual serving dishes. Spoon the marinade over them and sprinkle with the coconut. Serves 6.

Peach Cream Mold

Delicately rich but worth every calorie. I would have to play 36 holes of golf, carrying my bag, in order to have as large a serving of this as I would like.

2 packages unflavored gelatin
⅓ cup cold water
1 cup light cream
16 ounces cream cheese
2 cups heavy cream
1 cup sugar
10 ounces frozen, sliced peaches

Soften the gelatin in the ⅓ cup of cold water. Scald the 1 cup of light cream. Add the gelatin and stir until dissolved. Cool. Soften the cream cheese and beat until light. Add the 2 cups of heavy cream, beating constantly until smooth. Add the 1 cup of sugar. Purée the thawed sliced peaches. Add it to the cheese mixture. Combine the gelatin and cheese mixtures and pour into a melon mold. Refrigerate for several hours until set. Serves 10 to 12.

Baked Pears

1 can pears, save juice	1 cup heavy cream
butter	6 tablespoons icing sugar
dark brown sugar	⅓ cup dry sherry
dry white wine	nutmeg

Arrange the canned pear halves in a buttered shallow baking dish, sliced side up. Dot the pears with the butter and sprinkle with the dark brown sugar. Use half the amount of pear juice and add an equal amount of the dry white wine. Pour this over the pears. Bake in a 400° oven until the pears are light brown in color. For the sauce, beat the 1 cup of heavy cream with the icing sugar until stiff. Fold in the sherry and sprinkle with a little nutmeg. Serve the pears warm accompanied by this sauce. Serves 4 to 6.

Raspberry Soufflé

1 package frozen raspberries
1 envelope gelatin
¼ cup cold water
4 eggs, separated
¾ cup sugar
pinch of salt
1 cup heavy cream, whipped

Thaw the raspberries and work them through a sieve, or blend them in a blender and strain the seeds. Sprinkle the gelatin over the ¼ cup of cold water to soften it. In the top of a double boiler, beat the egg yolks lightly and gradually beat in ½ cup of the sugar and the salt. Reserve the remaining ¼ cup of sugar for the egg whites. Cook over simmering water, stirring constantly until it is thickened. Remove from the heat and stir in the gelatin until it is dissolved. Let stand until cool but not set. Stir in the raspberry purée. Beat the egg whites until frothy. Gradually beat in the ¼ cup of sugar and beat until stiff. Gently fold this meringue and the whipped cream into the raspberry mixture. Pour into a soufflé dish and chill for about 4 hours. Serves 6 to 8.

Fresh Strawberries with Wine Sauce

The flavor of the strawberry is brought out delicately when you prepare it this way.

1 to 2 pounds strawberries
¾ cup port or red wine
3 tablespoons berry sugar
1 orange, rind and juice
¼ cup red currant jelly
whipping cream

Hull the strawberries, wash them quickly if necessary, and place into a serving bowl. Boil the wine until reduced by half. Add the sugar, grated rind, and juice of 1 orange. Remove from the heat and add the red currant jelly, stirring until it is melted. When quite cold, pour this sauce over the strawberries and chill well. Serve with slightly whipped cream.

Tunnel Cake

This was the first party dessert I ever attempted when I was newly married. I was terrified to cut it and so relieved when the first piece came out so easily. It looked so attractive. And I was just thrilled when the guest of honor asked for seconds!

½ pound marshmallows (32)
¼ teaspoon salt
⅓ cup water
6 ounces semi-sweet chocolate bits
1 cup cream, whipped
⅛ teaspoon almond extract
10 inch orange chiffon or angel food cake
whipped cream (for frosting)

Combine the marshmallows, salt, and water in the top of a double boiler. Place it over gently boiling water and heat until the contents are melted, stirring frequently. Remove from the heat and stir in the semi-sweet chocolate bits. Chill about 10 minutes. Fold in the 1 cup whipped cream and the almond extract. Cut the top (1 inch) off the chiffon cake, and put it aside. Hollow out a trench in the cake and tear slightly the pieces of cake that have been removed from the trench. Fill the trench with ½ of the filling, followed by the torn pieces of cake. Spread the rest of the filling over the cake's surface, and replace the top that was originally cut off. Frost the sides with additional whipped cream. Serves 10.

Helpful Hints

Helpful Hints for Appetizers:

1. To blanch almonds, pour boiling water over them and let them stand for five minutes, then the skins will slip off easily.
2. For a quick first course try half an avocado with a spoon of sour cream in the center, topped with a bit of red caviar.
3. Dip a water chestnut in Parmesan cheese then wrap it with bacon. Secure with a toothpick and bake in a 400° oven until the bacon is cooked. Delicious!
4. Mix equal amounts of Parmesan cheese and mayonnaise and spread on Norwegian flat bread. Sprinkle with paprika and heat in a 325° oven for 3 to 4 minutes or until lightly browned.

Helpful Hints for Soups:

1. If too much salt has been added to soups or stews, add a potato. It will absorb the salt.
2. To help keep soup hot, serve it at the table from a heated tureen and use warm soup plates. Always serve hot soups really hot.

Helpful Hints for Salads and Salad Dressings:

1. For patio entertaining, serve jello molds in paper cups.
2. Salad is supposed to be served cold on cold plates. I have glass salad plates which I put into the freezer a few hours before dinner, so when they are placed in front of guests, they have a frosted look.
3. Cut out the core of a head of lettuce, wash the head under cold water, drain and wrap it in paper towels which have been moistened with cold water, and it will stay nice and crisp.
4. It takes four people to make a salad—a spendthrift for the oil, a miser for the vinegar, a counselor for the salt, and a madman to stir them up.
5. Dressing should not be added to salad until the last minute because the oil causes lettuce to wilt.
6. To keep celery crisp, wash and cut an Irish potato into small pieces and drop them into the container holding the celery. Fill the container with water and some ice. Cover it and keep in the fridge. The celery will be very crisp.

Helpful Hints for Sauces:

1. For an easy and delicious cheese sauce, make an ordinary white sauce and add 2 tablespoons of Cheez Whiz or sufficient to suit your taste.
2. One tablespoon of cornstarch is equivalent in thickening to one egg.
3. For a 'hurry up' chocolate sauce, melt some Hershey milk chocolate with almonds over hot water, then stir in a tablespoon of rum. Serve warm over vanilla ice cream.

Helpful Hints for Seafood

1. To improve canned shrimp, soak them in ice water for 1 hour before using.
2. Herbs and spices, if not used with care, can sometimes overpower the natural flavor of vegetables, meats, and fish.
3. Fish is often ruined by using too high a heat and for too long a period. Over cooked fish is tasteless and dry. We are fortunate to have a good friend who loves fishing and often presents us with fresh fish, but always with the caution, "If you over cook it, I won't bring you any more."
4. Fresh fish should be kept very cold and used as soon as possible.
5. Add some chopped capers and a bit of lemon juice to mayonnaise as a nice accompaniment to fish.

Helpful Hints for Meats:

1. To keep stuffed green peppers in shape while baking them, place them into muffin tins.
2. Add a little soft bread crumbs to hamburger steak to make it more tender.
3. Rub steaks, chops, or roasts with French dressing and let them stand at least two hours—this will help tenderize them.
4. Do not salt meat until ready to cook it. Salt tends to draw out the juices.
5. Have you ever tried a few drops of Worcestershire sauce on bacon before broiling it? Mighty tasty. I have a brother who sprinkles it on his CNR crusty buns (CPR in the west) after he butters them with nice hard butter.
6. Your roasts, steaks, and chops will be more tender if they are cooked at room temperature rather than taken right from the fridge.
7. Good digestion follows slow eating.
8. Pork is not easily digested, therefore it should be thoroughly cooked before serving.
9. When warming leftover meat, place it into a heavy skillet and cover completely with lettuce leaves. Cover tightly and heat in a moderate oven. This produces a nice moist meat which tastes as though it was just made.
10. When making ground beef patties, add grated zucchini instead of bread crumbs. The patties have a much better texture and flavor.
11. Try dredging slices of calves' liver in grated Parmesan cheese before you sauté it.
12. A mixture of honey and mustard makes a great last minute glaze for pork or spareribs.
13. Rolled rib roast is great for a large crowd because of its shape—one end is larger than the other. This means that one end is better cooked than the other, so you can please everyone.

Helpful Hints for Poultry and Game:

1. Soak chicken livers in milk for a half hour before cooking. It improves their flavor.
2. The secret of a good curry is the long frying of curry powder.

Helpful Hints for Eggs and Cheese:

1. A little vinegar added to the water when poaching eggs prevents the egg whites from spreading.
2. To keep cheese from becoming hard, wrap it in cloth which has been moistened in vinegar.
3. For an easy luncheon or supper dish, wrap large firm bananas in slices of cold ham topped with slices of processed cheese. These are broiled until the cheese starts to melt. Serve them hot. Children love them.

Helpful Hints for Vegetables:

1. When cooking cabbage, boil it in a bit of water for 10 minutes, then drain. Replace the water with milk and continue cooking until soft. This eliminates some of the unpleasant side effects that cabbage can produce and also improves the flavor.
2. People who do not normally like turnip will enjoy it if you add a few tablespoons of applesauce, a bit of brown sugar, and a small glob of butter. As this is a dish that is often served with turkey (out west anyway) I make a large dish the day before and put it into the refrigerator. The next day, I put buttered crumbs on and just bake until the crumbs are brown.
3. Peeling onions will cause you to shed a tear or two unless you peel them under cold running water. To remove the unpleasant after-odor, rub your hands with vinegar or lemon juice.
4. Vegetables grown below the surface of the soil contain valuable mineral salts in the skins. Scrub the skins rather than peeling them whenever possible.
5. To remove the skins from tomatoes, put them into boiling water for 1 minute—do only two at a time. Put them into the refrigerator to firm them for slicing etc.
6. To cook asparagus, clean then tie them together in a bunch and place them upright in the lower part of a double boiler. Add water to within 2 inches of the tips. Cover with the inverted top of the double boiler. The lower part of the stalks will cook while the tips steam without getting mushy. Do not over cook.
7. If you prefer soft skins on your baked potatoes, immerse them in hot water for 15 minutes before baking.
8. To keep spaghetti and macaroni from boiling over, put a tablespoon of oil in the water.
9. Half a cup of milk added to the water in which cauliflower is cooking helps to keep the cauliflower white.
10. French fry carrots like potatoes—they're very tasty.
11. Stir a little mint jelly into cooked green peas.
12. For a glossy finish to sautéed mushrooms, add a little lemon juice to the butter.

13. Roasted potatoes will have a better appearance and texture if you parboil them first (about 5 minutes). If you are cooking more than will fit easily around the roast, put them into a pan with a mixture of oil and butter, and sprinkle them with salt, pepper, and paprika. Bake them for about 1 hour in a 350° oven, turning them half way through the cooking, or when they are nicely browned on the bottom.

Helpful Hints for Breads:

1. When making muffins, make a double batch and put the second batch into the freezer. When you next want muffins, place the frozen muffins into a tightly covered pan and heat them in a slow oven. They'll taste freshly baked.
2. When baking loaf cakes, let the batter sit in the pan for twenty minutes before baking. This will lessen the size of the crack so typical of loaf cakes.
3. Soft bread cuts more easily with a slightly heated bread knife.

Helpful Hints for Cakes, Cookies, and Pies:

1. When melting chocolate, grease the container in which it is to be melted, and place it over boiling water.
2. When measuring molasses, grease the measuring cup first.
3. The layers of a cake will come out of the pans without sticking if you set the cake pans on a damp cloth as soon as you remove them from the oven.
4. When baking chocolate cakes, grease the pans then dust them with cocoa instead of flour.
5. When cutting meringue, a well greased knife does a tidier job.
6. To keep egg whites from falling, add a pinch of cream of tartar when beating.
7. Store all broken cookies and cookie crumbs in a sealed container. Use as a pie crust by blending 1½ cups crushed crumbs with ⅓ cup melted butter and pressing into the bottom of a pie plate. Chill and fill with pie filling.
8. Sprinkle a little wheat germ on fruit pies during the last 10 minutes of baking time. It produces a nutlike flavor.
9. Fifteen square graham crackers equal 1 cup of crumbs.

Helpful Hints for Desserts:

1. Apples and potatoes, when peeled, cored, and sliced, will not turn black if immediately placed in cold salted water.
2. If butter is rubbed around the top of the saucepan in which you are making fudge, it will prevent it from boiling over.
3. Spoon a bit of frozen orange juice (undiluted) over cut up fresh fruit for a deliciously refreshing fruit salad.
4. Soften 1 quart of vanilla ice cream with a small can of frozen limeade and spoon into a graham cracker pie crust. Sprinkle with finely grated lime peel and freeze.
5. Blueberry pie filling makes an easy and attractive topping for cheesecake.

Suggested Menus

The number of people that most of these recipes will serve is approximate, as so much depends on appetite and the rest of the menu. If you are entertaining a group of teenagers, expect that they will eat considerably more than the over forty group.

Suggested Menus for 4 to 6 people:

* Can be made the day before
** Can be made the morning of
*** Can be made ahead and frozen

Number 1

Crocked Cheese * p. 15
Brown Soup * p. 30 with Parmesan Fingers *** p. 136
Tossed green salad with Creamy Anchovy Garlic Dressing (make dressing ahead)
    p. 51
Steak Diane p. 71
Broccoli with Cream Sauce (make sauce and crumbs the morning of) p. 113
Tomatoes with Chopped Mushroom Filling (make filling ahead) p. 130
Raspberry Soufflé * p. 174
Suggested wine: Full bodied young red e.g. Barolo (Italy), Cabernet Sauvignon
                (California)

Number 2

Country Pâté p. 23 with Cumberland Sauce * p. 57
Caesar Salad (wash and dry lettuce and have all ingredients assembled) p. 42
Salmon Steaks (Broil 2 inches from heat for 4 minutes each side or until fish
                flakes easily with a fork but is still moist. Baste once on each
                side with melted butter.)
Spinach Royale ** p. 127
Rice or small parsleyed new potatoes
Frozen Lemon Soufflé *** p. 172
Suggested wine: White Burgundy e.g. Riesling (Alsace or California)

Number 3

Pâté à La Maison * p. 24
Crème Crécy (Cream of Carrot Soup) * p. 34
Tossed green salad
Pork Tenderloin with Orange Sauce p. 82
Baked Acorn Squash Rings filled with peas (prepare squash rings the morning of)
    p. 127
Rice p. 124
Almond Crisps (make cookies ahead but don't fill until shortly before) p. 163
Suggested wine: White German

Number 4

Shrimp Bisque with Shrimp Balls * p. 37
Bean Sprout and Spinach Salad p. 42
Sole and Crab in Silver Triangles ** p. 66
Baked Tomatoes with Cornflake Topping (make topping ahead) p. 129
Parsleyed Rice
Orange Bavarian Cream p. 173
Suggested wine: White Burgundy e.g. Pinot Chardonnay (California)

Number 5

Oysters Rockefeller (make spinach base and sauce ahead) p. 22
Tomato Bouillon * p. 38
Beef Tenderloin Steak with Red Wine and Pimentos p. 71
Puffy Parmesan Cauliflower p. 116
Mixture of green peas and pea pods, or
Baked Cherry Tomatoes (prepare tomatoes ahead but don't bake until ready to
serve) p. 128
No-Bake Cheesecake *** p. 167
Suggested wine: Red of any kind

Suggested Menus for 8 people:

* Can be made the day before
** Can be made the morning of
*** Can be made ahead and frozen

Number 1

Cheese Squares *** (bake just before serving) p. 14
Clam Chowder * p. 31
Bean Sprout and Spinach Salad ** (Make dressing and other ingredients the
morning of, but do not toss until last
minute.) p. 42
Baked Whole Salmon with Egg Sauce (Make egg sauce ahead and heat before
serving. Prepare fish, wrap in foil and
have it 'oven-ready'.) p. 61
Small parsleyed new potatoes
Herb Scalloped Tomatoes ** p. 130
Mixture of Peas and Pea Pods (Boil peas, drain, butter and mix with pea
pods, which have been stir-fried in a bit of
butter just until they are heated through.)
Frozen Lemon Soufflé *** p. 172
Suggested wine: White Burgundy e.g. Riesling (Alsace or California)

Number 2

Joyce's Golden Olive Nuggets * (bake before serving) p. 18
Shellfish Casserole * (can be made oven-ready the morning of, or the night
          before) p. 65
Rice p. 124
Tomato Gelatin Salad * p. 48
Tossed green salad
Fresh Strawberries with Wine Sauce, p. 175 or
Orange Slices in Curaçao p. 173
Suggested wine: Dry White e.g. Sauvignon, Sylvaner

Number 3

Clam Savories * p. 16
Roast Leg of New Zealand Lamb p. 80
Green Peas (add a bit of mint jelly to cooked peas)
Potatoes Romanoff * p. 122
Baked Tomatoes with Cornflake Topping ** (can be assembled ahead of time
          but not baked) p. 129
Annie's Cheesecake ***
*Suggested wine: Red Bordeaux e.g. Rioja (Spain), Cabernet Sauvignon (Calif-
ornia), Valpolicella (Italy)*

Number 4

Bacon and Cheese Appetizer * p. 11
Tray of celery and assorted olives
Chicken in Orange (doubled) * (make partly the night before and partly the
          morning of) p. 95
Baked Rice p. 124
Baked Acorn Squash Rings p. 127
Orange Bavarian Cream * p. 173
Suggested wine: German White

Number 5

Assorted cheeses with Oat Biscuits * (make biscuits ahead) p. 21
Curried Chicken Balls * p. 16
Moussaka *** p. 77
Tossed green salad
Garlic Bread
Quick Blender Chocolate Mousse * (doubled) p. 169
Suggested wine: Full bodied red e.g. Chianti, California Pinot

Suggested Menus for 10 to 12 people:

* Can be made the day before
** Can be made the morning of
*** Can be made ahead and frozen

Number 1

Onion Squares p. 21
Chicken Baked in Foil ** p. 90
Broccoli Casserole * p. 112
Carrots Grand Marnier * p. 116
Tunnel Cake (serves 10) * p. 175, or
Rhubarb Cream Pie, (2 pies, each one serving 6) *** p. 161
Suggested wine: Any of your favorites

Number 2

Meat Empanadas *** p. 19
Marion's Lasagna * p. 76
Tossed green salad
Garlic Bread (have oven-ready the morning of)
Cheesecake *** p. 165
Suggested wine: Full bodied Italian red e.g. Barolo, Chianti

Number 3

Raw Vegetables with Spinach Dip * p. 26
Seafood Casserole (doubled) * p. 63
Rice p. 124
Orange and Onion Salad p. 46
Hot Rolls
Pecan Tarts * p. 160
Suggested wine: Dry White e.g. Sauvignon, Sylvaner

Number 4

Curried Shrimp Puffs (can be partially made ahead) p. 17
Chicken Breasts Mandolay (doubled) ** p. 93
Rice p. 124
French-style green beans
Tossed green salad
No-Bake Cheesecake *** p. 167
Suggested wine: Semi-sweet White e.g. Chemin Blanc (France, California)

Number 5

Marinated Shrimp * p. 19
Chicken and Broccoli Casserole * p. 91
Peachy Ginger Salad Mold * p. 47
Tossed green salad

Sherry Almond Pudding (10 servings) * p. 164, or
Lemon Tarts * p. 159
Suggested wine: Dry White e.g. Sylvaner, Sauvignon

Suggested Menus for 14 to 16 people:

* Can be made the day before
** Can be made the morning of
*** Can be made ahead and frozen

Number 1

Pickled Mushrooms * p. 25
Sherry Roast Pork Parkins (Use an 8 to 10 pound roast as there is a bit of
shrinkage in roast pork. Make the sauce ahead and
double it for the larger roast.) p. 83
Easy Potato Bake ** (No need to double, as not everyone eats potatoes.) p. 120
Carrots Grand Marnier p. 116
Peas (add a few chopped water chestnuts for interest)
Apple Pie ***
Suggested wine: Full-bodied White e.g. White Burgundy, Riesling (Alsace,
California), or Light Red e.g. Valpolicella (Italy), Rioja (Spain)

Number 2

Tangy Cheese Balls *** p. 14
Curried Chicken * p. 98
Rice p. 124
Puppodums (green oval container found in specialty food section—contains
little rounds of Indian bread which are flat before cooking, but
once fried, take on all sorts of interesting shapes)
Condiments (use those suggested in Curried Chicken recipe)
Baked Pears p. 174, or
White Grapes with Sour Cream * p. 170
Suggested wine: Semi-sweet White e.g. Chemin Blanc (France, California),
German White

Number 3

Meat Samosa *** p. 20
Victor's Chicken * p. 99
Rice p. 124, or Lynn's Parmesan Spaghetti p. 125
Tossed green salad
Pecan Pie *** p. 160
Suggested wine: as for other chicken dishes

Suggested Menus for 20 to 25 people:

* Can be made the day before
** Can be made the morning of
*** Can be made ahead and frozen

Number 1

Country Pâté * p. 23
Rolled rib roast (Buy the whole roast, usually around 16 to 18 pounds. Cook in
a 325° oven. Times are approximate—for rare, 15 to 18
minutes per pound; for medium, 20 to 22 minutes per pound;
for well done, don't do it to a beautiful roast like this! Buy a
cheaper cut like rump roast and cook 30 to 35 minutes per
pound.)
Mary's Broccoli Casserole * p. 113
Scalloped Onions ** p. 118
Baked Tomatoes (use either topping) ** p. 129
Cheesecake (you will need 2) *** p. 165
Suggested wine: best Red available

Number 2

Cheese Ball * p. 11, 13
Chilean Chicken (serve extra sauce) * p. 97
Rice p. 124
Green peas with sautéed fresh mushrooms
Tossed green salad, or Creamy Cole Slaw p. 43
Carrot Cake *** p. 141
Suggested wine: as for other chicken dishes

Number 3

Camembert and Butter Ball * p. 11
Sirloin roast of beef (Allow ½ pound per person. Rub well with dry mustard,
salt, and pepper, and insert slivers of garlic into fat. It is
safest to use meat thermometer: for rare, internal temper-
ature should be 140°, for medium, 160°, for well done,
170°.)
Potatoes Milano ** p. 121
Carrot Asparagus Casserole ** p. 115
Tossed green salad
Chocolate Mousse * p. 168
Suggested wine: best Red available

Metric Conversion Chart

Equipment:

1 teaspoon	5 ml (milliliters)
1 tablespoon (3 teaspoons)	15 ml
1/4 cup (4 tablespoons)	60 ml
1/3 cup (5 1/3 tablespoons)	79 ml
1/2 cup (8 tablespoons)	118 ml
1 cup (16 tablespoons)	237 ml
1 fluid ounce (2 tablespoons)	30 ml
8 fluid ounces (1 cup)	237 ml
16 fluid ounces (1 pint)	473 ml
32 fluid ounces (1 quart)	946 ml

Dry Measure:

0.035 ounces	1.0 g (gram)
1 ounce	28.35 g
1 pound	453.59 g or 0.45 kg (kilograms)
2.21 pounds	1 kg

How to Convert to Metric:

	When You Know:	**You Can Find:**	**If You Multiply By:**
Mass:	ounces	grams	28.0
	pounds	kilograms	0.45
Liquid Volume:	ounces	milliliters	30.0
	pints	liters	0.47
	quarts	liters	0.95
	gallons	liters	3.8
Temperature:	degrees F	degrees C	5/9 after subtracting 32

Sample Temperature Conversions:

Degrees Fahrenheit:	**Degrees Celsius:**
225	107
250	121
275	135
300	149
350	177
400	204
450	232
500	260

Index